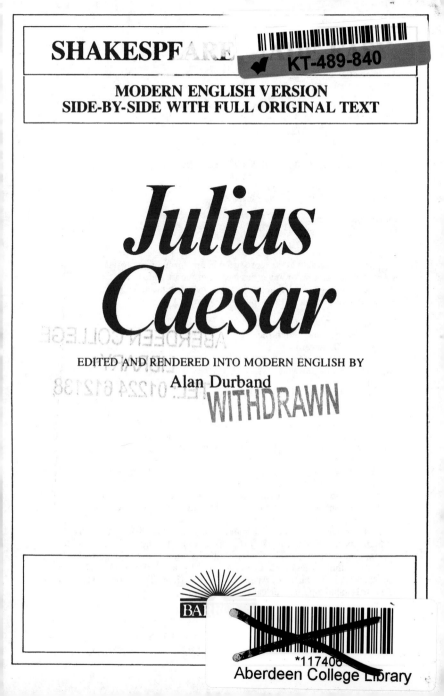

# SHAKESPEARE

## MODERN ENGLISH VERSION
## SIDE-BY-SIDE WITH FULL ORIGINAL TEXT

# *Julius Caesar*

EDITED AND RENDERED INTO MODERN ENGLISH BY

## Alan Durband

BA

First U.S. edition published 1985 by
Barron's Educational Series, Inc.

Hutchinson & Co. (Publishers) Ltd
An imprint of the Hutchinson Publishing Group
17-21 Conway Street, London W1P 6JD

Hutchinson Publishing Group (Australia) Pty Ltd
PO Box 496, 16-22 Church Street, Hawthorne,
Melbourne, Victoria 3122

Hutchinson Group (NZ) Ltd
32-34 View Road, PO Box 40-086, Glenfield, Auckland 10

Hutchinson Group (SA) (Pty) Ltd
PO Box 337, Bergvlei 2012, South Africa

First published 1984
© Alan Durband 1984

*All inquiries should be addressed to:*
Barron's Educational Series, Inc.
250 Wireless Boulevard
Hauppauge, NY 11788
http://www.barronseduc.com

ISBN-13: 978-0-8120-3573-5
ISBN-10: 0-8120-3573-9

Library of Congress Catalog No. 84-28295

**Library of Congress Cataloging in Publication Data**
Shakespeare, William, 1564–1616.
    Julius Caesar.
    (Shakespeare made easy)
    Summary: Presents the original text of Shakespeare's play side by side with a
modern version, discusses the author and the theater of his time, and provides
quizzes and other study activities.
    1. Caesar, Julius – Drama.  2. Shakespeare, William, 1564–1616. Julius Caesar.
3. Shakespeare, William, 1564–1616—Study and teaching.  4. Caesar, Julius, in
fiction, drama, poetry, etc. [1. Caesar, Julius—Drama.  2. Shakespeare, William,
1564–1616. Julius Caesar.  3. Plays.  4. Shakespeare, William, 1564–1616—Study
and teaching.]  I. Durband, Alan.  II. Title.  III. Series: Shakespeare, William,
1564–1616. Shakespare made easy.
PR2808.A25    1985    822.3'3    84-28295
ISBN 0-8120-3573-9

PRINTED IN THE UNITED STATES OF AMERICA

60  59  58  57  56  55  54  53  52  51

'Reade him, therefore; and againe, and againe: And if then you do not like him, surely you are in some danger, not to understand him. . . .'

John Hemming
Henry Condell

*Preface to the 1623 Folio Edition*

# Shakespeare Made Easy

Titles in the series

# Contents

# Introduction

*Shakespeare Made Easy* is intended for readers approaching the plays for the first time, who find the language of Elizabethan poetic drama an initial obstacle to understanding and enjoyment. In the past, the only answer to the problem has been to grapple with the difficulties with the aid of explanatory footnotes (often missing when they are most needed) and a stern teacher. Generations of students have complained that "Shakespeare was ruined for me at school."

Usually a fuller appreciation of Shakespeare's plays comes in later life. Often the desire to read Shakespeare for pleasure and enrichment follows from a visit to the theater, where excellence of acting and production can bring to life qualities which sometimes lie dormant on the printed page.

*Shakespeare Made Easy* can never be a substitute for the original plays. It cannot possibly convey the full meaning of Shakespeare's poetic expression, which is untranslatable. *Shakespeare Made Easy* concentrates on the dramatic aspect, enabling the novice to become familiar with the plot and characters, and to experience one facet of Shakespeare's genius. To know and understand the central issues of each play is a sound starting point for further exploration and development.

Discretion can be used in choosing the best method to employ. One way is to read the original Shakespeare first, ignoring the modern version – or using it only when interest or understanding flags. Another way is to read the translation first, to establish confidence and familiarity with plot and characters.

Either way, cross-reference can be illuminating. The modern text can explain what is being said if Shakespeare's language is particularly complex or his expression antiquated. The Shakespeare text will show the reader of the modern paraphrase how much more can be expressed in poetry than in prose.

The use of *Shakespeare Made Easy* means that the newcomer need never be overcome by textual difficulties. From first to last, a measure of understanding is at hand – the key is provided for what has been a locked door to many students in the past. And as understanding grows, so an awareness develops of the potential of language as a vehicle for philosophic and moral expression, beauty and the abidingly memorable.

Even professional Shakespearean scholars can never hope to arrive at a complete understanding of the plays. Each critic, researcher, actor or producer merely adds a little to the work that has already been done, or makes fresh interpretations of the texts for new generations. For everyone, Shakespearean appreciation is a journey. *Shakespeare Made Easy* is intended to help with the first steps.

# William Shakespeare

## His life

William Shakespeare was born in Stratford-on-Avon, Warwickshire, on April 23, 1564, the son of a prosperous wool and leather merchant. Very little is known of his early life. From parish records we know that he married Ann Hathaway in 1582, when he was eighteen, and she was twenty-six. They had three children, the eldest of whom died in childhood.

Between his marriage and the next thing we know about him, there is a gap of ten years. Probably he became a member of a traveling company of actors. By 1592 he had settled in London and had earned a reputation as an actor and playwright.

Theaters were then in their infancy. The first (called *The Theatre*) was built in 1576. Two more followed as the taste for theater grew: *The Curtain* in 1577 and *The Rose* in 1587. The demand for new plays naturally increased. Shakespeare probably earned a living adapting old plays and working in collaboration with others on new ones. Today we would call him a "freelance," since he was not permanently attached to one theater.

In 1594, a new company of actors, The Lord Chamberlain's Men, was formed, and Shakespeare was one of the shareholders. He remained a member throughout his working life. The company regrouped in 1603 and was renamed The King's Men, with James I as its patron.

Shakespeare and his fellow-actors prospered. In 1598 they built their own theater, *The Globe*, which broke away from the traditional rectangular shape of the inn and its yard (the early home of traveling bands of actors). Shakespeare described it in *Henry V* as "this wooden O," because it was circular.

Many other theaters were built by investors eager to profit from the new enthusiasm for drama. *The Hope*, *The Fortune*,

*The Red Bull* and *The Swan* were all open-air "public" theaters. There were also many "private" (or indoor) theaters, one of which (*The Blackfriars*) was purchased by Shakespeare and his friends because the child actors who performed there were dangerous competitors. (Shakespeare denounces them in *Hamlet*.)

After writing some thirty-seven plays (the exact number is something which scholars argue about), Shakespeare retired to his native Stratford, wealthy and respected. He died on his birthday, in 1616.

## His plays

Shakespeare's plays were not all published in his lifetime. None of them comes to us exactly as he wrote it.

In Elizabethan times, plays were not regarded as either literature or good reading matter. They were written at speed (often by more than one writer), performed perhaps ten or twelve times and then discarded. Fourteen of Shakespeare's plays were first printed in Quarto (17cm × 21cm) volumes, not all with his name as the author. Some were authorized (the "good" Quartos) and probably were printed from prompt copies provided by the theater. Others were pirated (the "bad" Quartos) by booksellers who may have employed shorthand writers or bought actors' copies after the run of the play had ended.

In 1623, seven years after Shakespeare's death, John Hemming and Henry Condell (fellow-actors and shareholders in The King's Men) published a collected edition of Shakespeare's works – thirty-six plays in all – in a Folio (21cm × 34cm) edition. From their introduction it would seem that they used Shakespeare's original manuscripts ("we have scarce received from him a blot in his papers") but the Folio volumes that still survive are not all exactly alike, nor are the plays printed as we know them today, with act and scene divisions and stage directions.

A modern edition of a Shakespeare play is the result of a great deal of scholarly research and editorial skill over several centuries. The aim is always to publish a text (based on the good and bad Quartos and the Folio editions) that most closely resembles what Shakespeare intended. Misprints have added to the problems, so some words and lines are pure guesswork. This explains why some versions of Shakespeare's plays differ from others.

## His theater

The first playhouse built as such in Elizabethan London, constructed in 1576, was *The Theatre*. Its co-founders were John Brayne, an investor, and James Burbage, a carpenter turned actor. Like the six or seven "public" (or outdoor) theaters which followed it over the next thirty years, it was situated outside the city, to avoid conflict with the authorities. They disapproved of players and playgoing, partly on moral and political grounds, and partly because of the danger of spreading the plague. (There were two major epidemics during Shakespeare's lifetime, and on each occasion the theaters were closed for lengthy periods.)

*The Theatre* was a financial success, and Shakespeare's company performed there until 1598, when a dispute over the lease of the land forced Burbage to take down the building. It was re-created in Southwark, as *The Globe*, with Shakespeare and several of his fellow-actors as the principal shareholders.

By modern standards, *The Globe* was small. Externally, the octagonal building measured less than thirty meters across, but in spite of this it could accommodate an audience of between two and three thousand people. (The largest of the three theaters at the National Theatre complex in London today seats 1160.)

Performances were advertised by means of playbills posted around the city, and they took place during the hours of daylight when the weather was suitable. A flag flew to show that all was well, to save playgoers a wasted journey.

*Interior of the Swan Theatre – from a pen and ink drawing made in 1596 (Mansell Collection)*

At the entrance, a doorkeeper collected one penny (about 60 cents today) for admission to the "pit" – a name taken from the old inn-yards, where bear-baiting and cock-fighting were popular sports. This was the minimum charge for seeing a play. The "groundlings," as they were called, simply stood around the three sides of the stage, in the open air. Those who were better off could pay extra for a seat under cover. Stairs led from the pit to three tiers of galleries around the walls. The higher one went, the more one paid. The best seats cost one shilling (or $7 today). In theaters owned by speculators like Francis Langley and Philip Henslowe, half the gallery takings went to the landlord.

A full house might consist of 800 groundlings and 1500 in the galleries, with a dozen more exclusive seats on the stage itself for the gentry. A new play might run for between six and sixteen performances; the average was about ten. As there were no breaks between scenes, and no intervals, most plays could be performed in two hours. A trumpet sounded three times before the play began.

The acting company assembled in the Tiring House at the rear of the stage. This was where they attired (or dressed) themselves: not in costumes representing the period of the play, but in Elizabethan doublet and hose. All performances were therefore in modern dress, though no expense was spared to make the stage costumes lavish. The entire company was male. By law actresses were not allowed, and female roles were performed by boys.

Access to the stage from the Tiring House was through two doors, one on each side of the stage. Because there was no front curtain, every entrance had to have its corresponding exit, so an actor killed on stage had to be carried off. There was no scenery: the audience used its imagination, guided by the spoken word. Storms and night scenes might well be performed on sunny days in mid-afternoon; the Elizabethan playgoer relied entirely on the playwright's descriptive skills to establish the dramatic atmosphere.

Once on stage, the actors and their expensive clothes were protected from sudden showers by a canopy, the underside of which was painted blue and spangled with stars to represent the heavens. A trapdoor in the stage made ghostly entrances and the gravedigging scene in *Hamlet* possible. Behind the main stage, in between the two entrance doors, there was a curtained area, concealing a small inner stage, useful for bedroom scenes. Above this was a balcony, which served for castle walls (as in *Henry V*) or a domestic balcony (as in the famous scene in *Romeo and Juliet*).

The acting style in Elizabethan times was probably more declamatory than we favor today, but the close proximity of the audience also made a degree of intimacy possible. In those days soliloquies and asides seemed quite natural. Act and scene divisions did not exist (those in printed versions of the play today have been added by editors), but Shakespeare often indicates a scene-ending by a rhyming couplet.

A company such as The King's Men at *The Globe* would consist of around twenty-five actors, half of whom might be shareholders, and the rest part-timers engaged for a particular play. Among the shareholders in *The Globe* were several specialists – William Kempe, for example, was a renowned comedian and Robert Armin was a singer and dancer. Playwrights wrote parts to suit the actors who were available, and devised ways of overcoming the absence of women. Shakespeare often has his heroines dress as young men, and physical contact between lovers was formal compared with the realism we expect today.

## His verse

Shakespeare wrote his plays mostly in blank verse: that is, unrhymed lines consisting of ten syllables, alternately stressed and unstressed. The technical term for this form is the iambic pentameter. When Shakespeare first began to write for the stage, it was fashionable to maintain this regular beat from the first line of the play till the last.

Shakespeare conformed at first and then experimented. Some of his early plays contain whole scenes in rhyming couplets – in *Romeo and Juliet*, for example, there is extensive use of rhyme, and as if to show his versatility, Shakespeare even inserts a sonnet into the dialogue.

But as he matured, he sought greater freedom of expression than rhyme allowed. Rhyme is still used to indicate a scene ending, or to stress lines which he wishes the audience to remember. Generally, though, Shakespeare moved toward the rhythms of everyday speech. This gave him many dramatic advantages, which he fully and subtly exploits in terms of atmosphere, character, emotion, stress and pace.

It is Shakespeare's poetic imagery, however, that most distinguishes his verse from that of lesser playwrights. It enables him to stretch the imagination, express complex thought-patterns in memorable language and convey a number of associated ideas in a compressed and economical form. A study of Shakespeare's imagery – especially in his later plays – is often the key to a full understanding of his meaning and purposes.

At the other extreme is prose. Shakespeare normally reserves it for servants, clowns, commoners and pedestrian matters such as lists, messages and letters.

# Julius Caesar

## Date

*Julius Caesar* was written in 1599. It was probably one of the first plays to be performed at the new Globe Theatre, the construction of which began in January of that year. The play was not published until 1623, when it appeared in the Folio Edition, complete with act (but not scene) divisions.

## Source

Shakespeare found the material for his plot in Sir Thomas North's translation of Plutarch's *Lives of the Noble Grecians and Romans*, which was first published in English in 1579 and reprinted in 1595.

The lives of Marcus Brutus, Julius Caesar and Marcus Antonius provided him with three approaches to his central theme, the assassination of Caesar in 44 B.C. Plutarch was a moral philosopher more than a historian, so Shakespeare learned a great deal about the characters of the three men, their motives, and their impact on other people. Plutarch's biographies are also the source of most of Shakespeare's other Roman plays.

There are several lines and passages in *Julius Caesar* which resemble North's vivid prose very closely, and a study of the three lives shows that Shakespeare retained much of the original character studies. But he was selective: he added, deleted and altered to suit his dramatic purposes, telescoping three years of history into six days of action. The speeches in the Forum have no historical precedent; the emotional and fickle mob is his own invention; the characters of Casca, Octavius, Portia and Calpurnia are greatly expanded. Shakespeare brought all the minor characters to life (they are mostly only mentioned by name in the original) and deftly wove them into the fabric of the play as a whole.

The raw material of *Julius Caesar* is indeed to be found in North's translation of Plutarch, but the finished product is entirely Shakespeare's. Other plays about Caesar were written in Elizabethan times, according to historical records, but none is thought to have been the precursor of *Julius Caesar* or to have influenced Shakespeare in writing his own version of the historical facts.

## Text

*Julius Caesar* was first printed in the Folio Edition of 1623, and scholars believe that the text used was originally a promptbook used in the theater, perhaps one preserved by the editors who would have known the play from its first performances. In *Act 4 Scene 3* there seems to be a duplication: the news of Portia's death is announced twice. Some editors think Shakespeare intended this. Others suggest that the second announcement is the one Shakespeare preferred and that the first ought to have been deleted. Apart from this, the text is one which scholars call "clean," that is to say, it is thought to be very close to Shakespeare's original manuscript.

# Julius Caesar

Original text and modern version

## The characters

**Julius Caesar**
**Octavius Caesar**
**Marcus Antonius** } triumvirs after the death of Julius Caesar
**M. Aemilius Lepidus**
**Cicero**
**Publius** } senators
**Popilius Lena**
**Marcus Brutus**
**Cassius**
**Casca**
**Trebonius**
**Caius Ligarius** } conspirators against Julius Caesar
**Decius Brutus**
**Metellus Cimber**
**Cinna**
**Flavius** and **Marullus**   tribunes   (elected representatives of
   the people)
**Artemidorus**   a teacher
**A Soothsayer**   (fortune-teller)
**Cinna**   a poet
**Another Poet**
**Lucilius**
**Titinius**
**Messala** } friends to Brutus and Cassius
**Young Cato**
**Volumnius**
**Varro**
**Clitus**
**Claudius** } servants or officers to Brutus
**Strato**
**Lucius**
**Dardanius**

**Pindarus**   servant to Cassius
**Commoners of Rome**   (Plebeians)
**Calpurnia**   wife to Caesar
**Portia**   wife to Brutus
**The Ghost of Caesar**
**Senators, Guards, Servants, Attendants, etc.**

# Act one

## Scene 1

*Rome. A street. Enter* **Flavius, Marullus** *and certain*
**Commoners.**

**Flavius**   Hence! home, you idle creatures, get you home:
Is this a holiday? What, know you not,
Being mechanical, you ought not walk
Upon a labouring day without the sign
5   Of your profession? Speak, what trade art thou?

**1st Commoner**   Why, sir, a carpenter.

**Marullus**   Where is thy leather apron, and thy rule?
What dost thou with thy best apparel on?
You, sir, what trade are you?

10 **2nd Commoner**   Truly, sir, in respect of a fine workman, I am
but, as you would say, a cobbler.

**Marullus**   But what trade art thou? Answer me directly.

**2nd Commoner**   A trade, sir, that I hope I may use with a safe
conscience;which is, indeed, sir, a mender of bad soles.

15 **Marullus**   What trade, thou knave? thou naughty knave, what
trade?

**2nd Commoner**   Nay, I beseech you, sir, be not out with me:
yet, if you be out, sir, I can mend you.

**Marullus**   What meanest thou by that? Mend me, thou saucy
20   fellow?

**2nd Commoner**   Why, sir, cobble you.

# Act one

## Scene 1

*A street in Rome.* **Flavius** *and* **Marullus**, *two tribunes, are trying to disperse a crowd of Roman workers, including a* **Carpenter** *and a* **Cobbler**.

**Flavius**   Go home, you idle wretches! Go home! Do you think today's a holiday? Don't you know you tradesmen should wear working clothes on weekdays? You – [*he questions the ringleader*] what's your trade?

**Carpenter**   Me, sir? I'm a carpenter.

**Marullus**   Then where's your leather apron and your ruler? What are you doing with your best clothes on? [*To another*] You there! What's your job?

**Cobbler**   To be honest, sir, compared with a real tradesman, I'm only what you'd call a mender or a cobbler.

**Marullus**   But what's your trade? A straight answer!

**Cobbler**   It's a trade I can follow with a clear conscience, sir. I'm a mender of bad soles.

**Marullus**   [*getting angry*] Your trade, idiot! You fool – what's your trade?

**Cobbler**   Please don't snap at me, sir! But should you snap, I can mend you!

**Marullus**   What do you mean by that? "Mend me," you impudent fellow?

**Cobbler**   Why, sir – cobble you.

**Flavius**    Thou art a cobbler, art thou?

**2nd Commoner**    Truly, sir, all that I live by is with the awl: I
    meddle with no tradesman's matters, nor women's matters;
25    but withal I am, indeed, sir, a surgeon to old shoes: when
    they are in great danger, I recover them. As proper men as
    ever trod upon neat's leather have gone upon my handiwork.

**Flavius**    But wherefore art not in thy shop today?
    Why dost thou lead these men about the streets?

30 **2nd Commoner**    Truly, sir, to wear out their shoes, to get
    myself into more work. But indeed, sir, we make holiday to
    see Caesar, and to rejoice in his triumph.

**Marullus**    Wherefore rejoice? What conquest brings he home?
    What tributaries follow him to Rome,
35    To grace in captive bonds his chariot wheels?
    You blocks, you stones, you worse than senseless things!
    O you hard hearts, you cruel men of Rome,
    Knew you not Pompey? Many a time and oft
    Have you climb'd up to walls and battlements,
40    To towers and windows, yea, to chimney-tops,
    Your infants in your arms, and there have sat
    The livelong day, with patient expectation,
    To see great Pompey pass the streets of Rome:
    And when you saw his chariot but appear,
45    Have you not made an universal shout,
    That Tiber trembled underneath her banks
    To hear the replication of your sounds
    Made in her concave shores?
    And do you now put on your best attire?
50    And do you now cull out a holiday?
    And do you now strew flowers in his way,
    That comes in triumph over Pompey's blood?
    Be gone!
    Run to your houses, fall upon your knees,

**Flavius**  [*understanding at last*] Oh, so you are a shoe repairer, are you?

**Cobbler**  Faith, sir: all my living is based on the awl. I don't meddle in tradesmen's affairs – nor in affairs with women – but, overall, I'm a shoe surgeon. When their lives are in danger, I save them. The finest men who ever wore shoe leather have trodden on my handiwork!

**Flavius**  But why aren't you in your workshop today? Why are you leading these men around the streets?

**Cobbler**  To wear their shoes out, sir – so I'll get more work! But joking apart, we've taken the day off to see Caesar and celebrate his victory.

**Marullus**  What is there to celebrate? What treasure has he brought back home? How many hostages has he fetched to Rome, chained to his chariot wheels, who'll pay us tribute money? Blockheads! Numskulls! Fools! Oh, you hard-hearted, cruel men of Rome! Don't you remember Pompey? Many a time you've climbed up walls and battlements, towers and windows, yes, even to the tops of chimneys, with your infants in your arms, sitting there patiently all the livelong day, to see great Pompey pass through the streets of Rome. And when you saw his chariot appear, didn't you all cheer together, making the River Tiber tremble beneath its banks when your cries echoed along its curving shores? And are you now sporting your best clothes? Making a public holiday for yourselves? Throwing flowers before the man who triumphed over Pompey's sons? Be off with you! Run home, fall on your

55  Pray to the gods to intermit the plague
    That needs must light on this ingratitude.

**Flavius**  Go, go, good countrymen, and for this fault
    Assemble all the poor men of your sort;
    Draw them to Tiber banks, and weep your tears
60  Into the channel, till the lowest stream
    Do kiss the most exalted shores of all.

*[Exeunt all the* **Commoners**]

See where their basest mettle be not mov'd;
They vanish tongue-tied in their guiltiness.
Go you down that way towards the Capitol;
65  This way will I. Disrobe the images,
    If you do find them deck'd with ceremonies.

**Marullus**  May we do so?
    You know it is the feast of Lupercal.

**Flavius**  It is no matter; let no images
70  Be hung with Caesar's trophies. I'll about
    And drive away the vulgar from the streets;
    So do you too, where you perceive them thick.
    These growing feathers pluck'd from Caesar's wing
    Will make him fly an ordinary pitch,
75  Who else would soar above the view of men
    And keep us all in servile fearfulness.

*[Exeunt]*

knees, and pray that the gods don't send a plague to punish you for this ingratitude!

**Flavius**   Go, fellow-countrymen, and to remedy this fault, gather together all the poor men of your class. Lead them to the banks of the Tiber, and cry there until your tears flood the river to its highest level.

[*The* **Commoners** *leave sheepishly*]

See how their ignorant feelings have been touched. They slink away, speechless with guilt. [*To* **Marullus**, *pointing*] You go down that way, toward the Capitol. I'll take this route. If you find any statues of Caesar with crowns or decorations on them, take them off.

**Marullus**   Dare we? You know it's the Feast of Lupercal.

**Flavius**   Who cares? No statues shall have Caesar's decorations on them. I'll go around ordering the common people off the streets. Do the same yourself, wherever you see them congregating. If we pull Caesar down a peg or two now, we'll maybe keep his feet on the ground. Left unchecked, he'll get above himself. We'll lose our freedom and live in fear.

[*They leave*]

## Scene 2

*A public place. Enter* **Caesar, Antony, Calpurnia, Portia, Decius, Cicero, Brutus, Cassius, Casca, a Soothsayer,** *and a crowd.*

**Caesar**    Calpurnia!

**Casca**                    Peace, ho! Caesar speaks.

**Caesar**                                        Calpurnia!

**Calpurnia**    Here, my lord.

**Caesar**    Stand you directly in Antonius' way
When he doth run his course. Antonius!

5 **Antony**    Caesar, my lord?

**Caesar**    Forget not, in your speed, Antonius,
To touch Calpurnia; for our elders say,
The barren touched in this holy chase,
Shake off their sterile curse.

**Antony**                    I shall remember:
10    When Caesar says, 'do this,' it is perform'd.

**Caesar**    Set on, and leave no ceremony out.

**Soothsayer**    Caesar!

**Caesar**    Ha! Who calls?

**Casca**    Bid every noise be still; peace yet again!

15 **Caesar**    Who is it in the press that calls on me?
I hear a tongue shriller than all the music
Cry 'Caesar!' Speak: Caesar is turn'd to hear.

**Soothsayer**    Beware the ides of March.

## Scene 2

*Rome: A public square crowded with Roman citizens celebrating the Feast of Lupercalia.* **Caesar** *enters ceremoniously, followed by his wife* **Calpurnia**, **Antony**, **Brutus** *and his wife* **Portia**, *and prominent Romans:* **Decius, Cicero, Casca, Cassius** *and others.* **Marullus** *and* **Flavius** *stand by, observing.*

**Caesar**   Calpurnia!

**Casca**   Silence! Caesar speaks!

**Caesar**   Calpurnia.

**Calpurnia**   I'm here, my lord.

**Caesar**   Stand directly in the way of Antony when he runs in the Lupercal race. Antony!

**Antony**   Caesar, my lord?

**Caesar**   In your haste, Antony, don't forget to touch Calpurnia. Our wise men say that to be touched during the race is a cure for sterility in women.

**Antony**   I shall remember. When Caesar says, "Do this!" it's done.

**Caesar**   Begin then, and leave no ceremony out.
[A **Soothsayer** *or* **Fortune-teller** *pushes his way through the crowd*]

**Fortune-teller**   Caesar!

**Caesar**   Hm? Who calls me?

**Casca**   Stop all this noise! Silence again!

**Caesar**   Who calls me from the crowd? I heard a voice rising above the music cry "Caesar." Speak! Caesar turns to listen.

**Fortune-teller**   Beware the ides of March! [*March 15*]      27

**Caesar**                                                What man is that?

**Brutus**    A soothsayer bids you beware the ides of March.

20 **Caesar**    Set him before me; let me see his face.

**Cassius**    Fellow, come from the throng; look upon Caesar.

**Caesar**    What say'st thou to me now? Speak once again.

**Soothsayer**    Beware the ides of March.

**Caesar**    He is a dreamer. Let us leave him. Pass.

[*Exeunt all except* **Brutus** *and* **Cassius**]

25 **Cassius**    Will you go see the order of the course?

**Brutus**    Not I.

**Cassius**                I pray you, do.

**Brutus**    I am not gamesome: I do lack some part
    Of that quick spirit that is in Antony.
    Let me not hinder, Cassius, your desires;
30    I'll leave you.

**Cassius**    Brutus, I do observe you now of late:
    I have not from your eyes that gentleness
    And show of love as I was wont to have.
    You bear too stubborn and too strange a hand
    Over your friend that loves you.

35 **Brutus**                                Cassius,
    Be not deceiv'd: if I have veil'd my look,
    I turn the trouble of my countenance
    Merely upon myself. Vexed I am
    Of late with passions of some difference,
40    Conceptions only proper to myself,
    Which give some soil, perhaps, to my behaviours;

28

**Caesar**   Who's that man?

**Brutus**   A fortune-teller advises you to beware of the ides of March.

**Caesar**   Bring him before me. Let me see his face.

**Cassius**   Fellow, come out of the crowd. Face Caesar.

**Caesar**   Now what have you to say to me? Repeat yourself.

**Fortune-teller**   Beware the ides of March.

**Caesar**   [*brushing him aside*] He is a dreamer. Let's leave him. Move on.

[*Trumpets sound. Everyone leaves except* **Brutus** *and* **Cassius**]

**Cassius**   Are you going to watch the race?

**Brutus**   Not me.

**Cassius**   Do, please . . .

**Brutus**   I'm not one for games. I haven't got Antony's lively character. Don't let me stop you, Cassius. I'll slip away.

**Cassius**   Brutus, I've been watching you lately. I can tell from your eyes that there's a coolness between us nowadays. You are too stiff and formal with your old friend.

**Brutus**   Cassius, don't be misled. If I look serious, I'm frowning at myself. Recently I've been at odds with myself over some personal matters, and it's affected my behavior. I don't want

But let not therefore my good friends be griev'd –
Among which number, Cassius, be you one –
Nor construe any further my neglect,
45    Than that poor Brutus, with himself at war,
Forgets the shows of love to other men.

**Cassius**    Then, Brutus, I have much mistook your passion;
By means whereof this breast of mine hath buried
Thoughts of great value, worthy cogitations.
50    Tell me, good Brutus, can you see your face?

**Brutus**    No, Cassius; for the eye sees not itself
But by reflection, by some other things.

**Cassius**    'Tis just;
And it is very much lamented, Brutus,
55    That you have no such mirrors as will turn
Your hidden worthiness into your eye,
That you might see your shadow. I have heard,
Where many of the best respect in Rome,
Except immortal Caesar, speaking of Brutus,
60    And groaning underneath this age's yoke,
Have wish'd that noble Brutus had his eyes.

**Brutus**    Into what dangers would you lead me, Cassius,
That you would have me seek into myself
For that which is not in me?

65 **Cassius**    Therefore, good Brutus, be prepar'd to hear;
And since you know you cannot see yourself
So well as by reflection, I, your glass,
Will modestly discover to yourself
That of yourself which you yet know not of.
70    And be not jealous on me, gentle Brutus:
Were I a common laugher, or did use
To stale with ordinary oaths my love
To every new protester; if you know

to upset my good friends – among whom I include you,
Cassius – nor have them think my aloofness has any
other reason than the conflict that is going on inside me. It
makes me unsociable.

**Cassius**    I've greatly misunderstood your mood then, Brutus,
and therefore kept my deep and innermost thoughts to
myself. [*He pauses, then decides to say more*] Tell me, good
Brutus: can you see your face?

**Brutus**    [*puzzled*] No, Cassius. The eye can only see itself by
reflection, with the help of other things.

**Cassius**    That's right! And it's greatly regretted, Brutus, that
you have no such mirror to see with your own eyes your own
inner qualities. I've heard many reputable Romans (except, of
course, immortal Caesar!) mention the name of Brutus when
complaining of the present tyranny. They've wished that
noble Brutus wasn't so blind.

**Brutus**    What dangers are you leading me into, Cassius, that
require me to search inside myself for things that are not
there?

**Cassius**    Good Brutus, bear with me while I explain. You know
you cannot see yourself except by reflection. I'll be your
mirror, then, and tell you faithfully things about yourself that
you yourself don't know. Don't be suspicious of me, Brutus. If I
were anybody's fool, or if I cheapened my friendship by
offering it to everyone, or if you think I fawn over men, then

31

That I do fawn on men and hug them hard,
75    And after scandal them; or if you know
That I profess myself in banqueting
To all the rout, then hold me dangerous.

[*Flourish and shout*]

**Brutus**    What means this shouting? I do fear the people
Choose Caesar for their king.

**Cassius**                                 Ay, do you fear it?
80    Then must I think you would not have it so.

**Brutus**    I would not, Cassius; yet I love him well.
But wherefore do you hold me here so long?
What is it that you would impart to me?
If it be aught toward the general good,
85    Set honour in one eye, and death i' th' other,
And I will look on both indifferently;
For let the gods so speed me as I love
The name of honour more than I fear death.

**Cassius**    I know that virtue to be in you, Brutus,
90    As well as I do know your outward favour.
Well, honour is the subject of my story.
I cannot tell what you and other men
Think of this life; but for my single self,
I had as lief not be as live to be
95    In awe of such a thing as I myself.
I was born free as Caesar; so were you;
We both have fed as well, and we can both
Endure the winter's cold as well as he:
For once, upon a raw and gusty day,
100    The troubled Tiber chafing with her shores,
Caesar said to me, 'Dar'st thou, Cassius, now
Leap in with me into this angry flood,

slander them afterward, or that I'm everybody's friend when I'm out drinking, then regard me as a dangerous man.

[*Trumpets sound and shouts are heard*]

**Brutus**   Why the shouting? I fear the people have chosen Caesar as their king!

**Cassius**   [*eagerly*] Yes? Do you fear it? Then I take it you wouldn't wish it to happen.

**Brutus**   I wouldn't, Cassius – yet I'm very fond of him. But why are you holding me here so long? What are you trying to tell me? If it's anything to do with the welfare of the people, show me honor on the one hand, and death on the other, and I'm indifferent either way. God knows I value my honor more than I fear death.

**Cassius**   I know that quality is within you, Brutus, as well as I recognize your looks. Well, honor is the subject of my story. I don't know what you and other men think of this life. For me, I'd just as soon be dead as be in awe of a fellow human being. I was born as free as Caesar. So were you. We've both been fed as well. We can both endure the cold of winter as well as he can. Once, on a cold and windy day, when the choppy Tiber was beating against its shores, Caesar said to me: "Cassius, I dare you to jump into this stormy sea with me and swim to

And swim to yonder point?' Upon the word,
Accoutred as I was, I plunged in
105   And bade him follow; so indeed he did.
The torrent roar'd, and we did buffet it
With lusty sinews, throwing it aside
And stemming it with hearts of controversy.
But ere we could arrive the point propos'd,
110   Caesar cried, 'Help me, Cassius, or I sink.'
I, as Aeneas, our great ancestor,
Did from the flames of Troy upon his shoulder
The old Anchises bear, so from the waves of Tiber
Did I the tired Caesar. And this man
115   Is now become a god, and Cassius is
A wretched creature, and must bend his body
If Caesar carelessly but nod on him.
He had a fever when he was in Spain,
And when the fit was on him, I did mark
120   How he did shake; 'tis true, this god did shake;
His coward lips did from their colour fly,
And that same eye whose bend doth awe the world
Did lose his lustre; I did hear him groan;
Ay, and that tongue of his, that bade the Romans
125   Mark him and write his speeches in their books,
Alas, it cried, 'Give me some drink, Titinius,'
As a sick girl. Ye gods, it doth amaze me
A man of such a feeble temper should
So get the start of the majestic world,
And bear the palm alone.

[*Flourish and shout*]

130 **Brutus**                        Another general shout?
I do believe that these applauses are
For some new honours that are heap'd on Caesar.

that point yonder!" That said, armored though I was, I plunged in and challenged him to follow. So indeed he did. The sea raged, and we fought against it with vigorous strokes, pushing the waves aside and overcoming the stream in our eager rivalry. But before we could reach the point we'd chosen, Caesar cried, "Help me, Cassius, or I'll drown." So, like our great ancestor Aeneas, who took old Anchises on his shoulders and rescued him from the flames of Troy, I saved the tired Caesar from the waves of the Tiber. And this same man is now become a god, whereas Cassius is a wretched nobody, who must bow if Caesar condescends to nod to him. He had a fever when he was in Spain, and at its height I noticed how he shook. It's true! This god actually shook! The blood drained from his cowardly lips, and that selfsame eye, whose stare awes the world, lost its sparkle. I heard him groan. Yes, and that tongue of his, that called on Romans to take heed of him and write down his speeches in their notebooks—alas, it cried, "Give me something to drink, Titinius," like a sick girl. Ye gods! It amazes me that a man so lacking in courage is able to outdistance the pack and become the emperor.

[*Shouts again: and the sounds of trumpets*]

**Brutus**   The crowd roars again! I believe the applause must be for some new honors lavished on Caesar.

**Cassius**    Why, man, he doth bestride the narrow world
Like a Colossus, and we petty men
135    Walk under his huge legs, and peep about
To find ourselves dishonourable graves.
Men at some time are masters of their fates:
The fault, dear Brutus, is not in our stars,
But in ourselves, that we are underlings.
140    Brutus and Caesar: what should be in that 'Caesar'?
Why should that name be sounded more than yours?
Write them together, yours is as fair a name;
Sound them, it doth become the mouth as well;
Weigh them, it is as heavy; conjure with 'em,
145    'Brutus' will start a spirit as soon as 'Caesar'.
Now in the names of all the gods at once,
Upon what meat doth this our Caesar feed,
That he is grown so great? Age, thou art sham'd!
Rome, thou hast lost the breed of noble bloods!
150    When went there by an age, since the great flood,
But it was fam'd with more than with one man?
When could they say, till now, that talk'd of Rome,
That her wide walks encompass'd but one man?
Now is it Rome indeed, and room enough,
155    When there is in it but one only man.
O, you and I have heard our fathers say,
There was a Brutus once that would have brook'd
Th' eternal devil to keep his state in Rome
As easily as a king.

160 **Brutus**    That you do love me, I am nothing jealous;
What you would work me to, I have some aim:
How I have thought of this, and of these times,
I shall recount hereafter. For this present,
I would not, so with love I might entreat you,
165    Be any further mov'd. What you have said
I will consider; what you have to say

**Cassius**    Why, man, he straddles the narrow world like the
Colossus of Rhodes, and we lesser men walk beneath his
huge legs, peeping around, going to our graves dishonored.
Men at some time are masters of their fates. The fault, dear
Brutus, is not in our stars but in ourselves, that we are inferior
in rank. Brutus and Caesar: what's so special about "Caesar"?
Why should that name be more famous than your own? Write
them side by side: yours is as good a name. Say them, and
each rolls of the tongue. Weigh them; they are of equal
weight. Conjure with them: "Brutus" will summon up a
supernatural spirit as effectively as "Caesar." In the name of
all the gods combined, what special meat does Caesar eat to
make him grow so great? It's a disgrace to our times! Rome—
you aren't making men of mettle any more! When was there a
time since the great flood that a generation produced only one
famous man? Whenever could it be said of Rome—till now—
that her wide walls encircled one man only? Rome is rightly
named, and room enough, when there's only one "Rome-
man" in it! Oh, you and I have heard our fathers say that there
was once a man called Brutus who would as soon have let the
devil reign in Rome, as tolerate a king.

**Brutus**    I do not doubt your high regard for me. I think I know
what you would have me do. Some other time, I'll tell you how
I've thought about this and the political situation generally.
But for now – if I can ask you as a friend – I'd prefer not to be
persuaded any further. What you have said, I'll consider. What

I will with patience hear, and find a time
Both meet to hear and answer such high things.
Till then, my noble friend, chew upon this:
170 Brutus had rather be a villager
Than to repute himself a son of Rome
Under these hard conditions as this time
Is like to lay upon us.

**Cassius**                    I am glad
That my weak words have struck but thus much show
175 Of fire from Brutus.

[*Enter* **Caesar** *and his train*]

**Brutus**   The games are done and Caesar is returning.

**Cassius**   As they pass by, pluck Casca by the sleeve,
And he will, after his sour fashion, tell you
What hath proceeded worthy note today.

180 **Brutus**   I will do so. But look you, Cassius,
The angry spot doth glow on Caesar's brow,
And all the rest look like a chidden train:
Calpurnia's cheek is pale, and Cicero
Looks with such ferret and such fiery eyes
185 As we have seen him in the Capitol,
Being cross'd in conference by some senators.

**Cassius**   Casca will tell us what the matter is.

**Caesar**   Antonius!

**Antony**                    Caesar?

**Caesar**   Let me have men about me that are fat,
190 Sleek-headed men, and such as sleep a-nights.
Yond Cassius has a lean and hungry look;
He thinks too much: such men are dangerous.

you'll say later, I'll listen to carefully and fix a suitable time for discussing such important matters. Meanwhile, my noble friend, turn this over in your mind: Brutus would rather be a peasant than a Roman citizen under the present oppressive regime.

**Cassius**  I'm glad that my little speech has sparked off such a show of spirit in you, Brutus.

[**Caesar** *enters, followed by his attendants*]

**Brutus**  The games have ended, and Caesar is returning.

**Cassius**  As they pass by, pull Casca by the sleeve. In his sour way, he'll tell you what notable things have happened today.

**Brutus**  I'll do that. But notice, Cassius, that Caesar's brow is flushed with anger and that all the others look embarrassed. Calpurnia's cheek is pale, and Cicero has that bloodshot look about his eyes he gets when senators argue with him in the Capitol.

**Cassius**  Casca will tell us what has happened.

**Caesar**  [*sharply*] Antony!

**Antony**  [*quick to respond*] Caesar?

**Caesar**  I want fat men around me, with smooth-combed hair, who sleep soundly at night. That Cassius has a lean and hungry look. He thinks too much. Such men are dangerous.

**Antony**    Fear him not, Caesar, he's not dangerous.
He is a noble Roman, and well given.

195 **Caesar**    Would he were fatter! But I fear him not:
Yet if my name were liable to fear,
I do not know the man I should avoid
So soon as that spare Cassius. He reads much,
He is a great observer, and he looks
200 Quite through the deeds of men. He loves no plays,
As thou dost, Antony; he hears no music.
Seldom he smiles, and smiles in such a sort
As if he mock'd himself, and scorn'd his spirit
That could be mov'd to smile at any thing.
205 Such men as he be never at heart's ease
Whiles they behold a greater than themselves,
And therefore are they very dangerous.
I rather tell thee what is to be fear'd
Than what I fear; for always I am Caesar.
210 Come on my right hand, for this ear is deaf,
And tell me truly what thou think'st of him.

[*Exeunt* **Caesar** *and his train*]

**Casca**    You pull'd me by the cloak. Would you speak with me?

**Brutus**    Ay, Casca. Tell us what hath chanc'd today,
That Caesar looks so sad.

215 **Casca**    Why, you were with him, were you not?

**Brutus**    I should not then ask Casca what had chanc'd.

**Casca**    Why, there was a crown offer'd him; and, being offer'd
him, he put it by with the back of his hand, thus; and then the
people fell a-shouting.

220 **Brutus**    What was the second noise for?

**Antony**   Have no fear of him, Caesar. He's not dangerous. He's a noble Roman, and no troublemaker.

**Caesar**   I wish he were fatter! But I'm not afraid of him. Yet if I were given to fear, there's no man I would more avoid than that skinny Cassius. He reads too much. He's very perceptive and good at analyzing motives. He's no playgoer as you are, Antony. He never listens to music. He seldom smiles, and when he does, he smiles as though in self-mockery, reproaching himself for ever smiling at anything. Men like him are never content while others rank above them. Therefore they are very dangerous. [*In case he's misunderstood*] I'm only telling you what might be feared, not what I fear, for I am Caesar, always. [*Beckoning to* **Antony**] Stand on my right – my left ear is deaf – and tell me honestly what you think of him.

[*They leave together, followed by Caesar's attendants*]

**Casca**   [*bluntly*] You pulled my cloak. Do you want to speak with me?

**Brutus**   Ay, Casca. What happened today to make Caesar look so grim?

**Casca**   Well, you were with him, were you not?

**Brutus**   I wouldn't be asking you what happened if I had been.

**Casca**   Well, they offered him a crown. And when it was offered, he brushed it aside with the back of his hand, like this. [**Casca** *demonstrates*] Then the people all shouted.

**Brutus**   What was the second noise for?

**Casca**    Why, for that too.

**Brutus**    They shouted thrice: what was the last cry for?

**Casca**    Why, for that too.

**Brutus**    Was the crown offer'd him thrice?

225 **Casca**    Ay, marry, was't, and he put it by thrice, every time gentler than other; and at every putting-by mine honest neighbours shouted.

**Cassius**    Who offered him the crown?

**Casca**    Why, Antony.

230 **Brutus**    Tell us the manner of it, gentle Casca.

**Casca**    I can as well be hang'd as tell the manner of it: it was mere foolery; I did not mark it. I saw Mark Antony offer him a crown; yet 'twas not a crown neither, 'twas one of these coronets; and, as I told you, he put it by once; but for all that,
235 to my thinking, he would fain have had it. Then he offered it to him again; then he put it by again; but to my thinking, he was very loath to lay his fingers off it. And then he offered it the third time. He put it the third time by; and still as he refus'd it, the rabblement hooted, and clapp'd their chopt
240 hands, and threw up their sweaty night-caps, and uttered such a deal of stinking breath because Caesar refus'd the crown, that it had, almost, choked Caesar; for he swounded, and fell down at it. And for mine own part, I durst not laugh, for fear of opening my lips and receiving the bad air.

245 **Cassius**    But soft, I pray you; what, did Caesar swound?

**Casca**    He fell down in the market-place, and foam'd at mouth, and was speechless.

**Brutus**    'Tis very like; he hath the falling-sickness.

**Casca**    For the same reason.

**Brutus**    They shouted three times. What was the last cry for?

**Casca**    Why, the same again.

**Brutus**    Was the crown offered to him three times?

**Casca**    Yes, indeed it was. And he put it aside three times, each time more gently than the last. And at every putting aside, my honest fellow-citizens shouted.

**Cassius**    Who offered him the crown?

**Casca**    Why, Antony.

**Brutus**    Tell us how, gentle Casca.

**Casca**    [*blunt as ever*] I'm hanged if I can describe it properly. It was all tomfoolery. I took no notice. I saw Mark Antony offer him a crown. Well, it wasn't really a crown, it was one of those laurel wreaths. And as I told you, he set it aside the first time. Mind you, I think he wanted to have it. Then Antony offered it to him again. He pushed it aside again. In my opinion, he was very reluctant to let go of it. And then Antony offered it a third time. He turned it away the third time. And as he continued to refuse it, the mob hooted and clapped their rough hands, and threw their sweaty nightcaps in the air, and delivered so much stinking breath because Caesar had refused the crown that it almost choked Caesar. He fainted and collapsed at the smell. For myself, I didn't dare laugh in case I opened my mouth and breathed the stench.

**Cassius**    But one moment, please . . . Did Caesar faint?

**Casca**    He fell down in the marketplace and foamed at the mouth and was speechless.

**Brutus**    Very likely. He suffers from falling-sickness [epilepsy].

**Cassius**    No, Caesar hath it not; but you, and I,
250    And honest Casca, we have the falling-sickness.

**Casca**    I know not what you mean by that, but I am sure Caesar
fell down. If the tag-rag people did not clap him and hiss him,
according as he pleas'd and displeas'd them, as they use to do
the players in the theatre, I am no true man.

255 **Brutus**    What said he when he came unto himself?

**Casca**    Marry, before he fell down, when he perceiv'd the
common herd was glad he refus'd the crown, he pluck'd me
ope his doublet, and offer'd them his throat to cut. And I had
been a man of any occupation, if I would not have taken him
260    at a word, I would I might go to hell among the rogues. And so
he fell. When he came to himself again, he said, if he had done
or said anything amiss, he desir'd their worships to think it
was his infirmity. Three or four wenches, where I stood,
cried, 'Alas, good soul,' and forgave him with all their hearts;
265    but there's no heed to be taken of them; if Caesar had stabb'd
their mothers, they would have done no less.

**Brutus**    And after that, he came, thus sad, away?

**Casca**    Ay.

**Cassius**    Did Cicero say anything?

270 **Casca**    Ay, he spoke Greek.

**Cassius**    To what effect?

**Casca**    Nay, and I tell you that, I'll ne'er look you i' th' face
again. But those that understood him smil'd at one another,
and shook their heads; but for mine own part, it was Greek to
275    me. I could tell you more news too: Marullus and Flavius, for
pulling scarfs off Caesar's images, are put to silence. Fare you
well. There was more foolery yet, if I could remember it.

**Cassius**    Will you sup with me tonight, Casca?

**Cassius**   No – not Caesar. It's you and I and honest Casca who have this falling-sickness!

**Casca**   I don't know what you mean by that remark, but Caesar certainly fell down. If the rabble didn't cheer him or hiss him according to whether he pleased or displeased them (as they applaud actors in the theater), call me a liar.

**Brutus**   What did he say when he came to?

**Casca**   Well, before he fell down – when he realized the mob was glad he turned down the crown – he loosened his collar and offered them his throat to cut. And if I had been a craftsman with a proper tool to use as a weapon, may I go to hell with the sinners if I would not have taken him at his word. And so he fell. When he came to, he said if he'd done or said anything improper, he hoped that the gentlemen would blame his infirmity. Three or four young women, where I stood, cried: "Alas, pour soul!" and forgave him with all their hearts. But take no notice of them. If Caesar had stabbed their mothers, they'd have said the same.

**Brutus**   And after that, he came away displeased?

**Casca**   Yes.

**Cassius**   Did Cicero say anything?

**Casca**   Yes. He spoke in Greek.

**Cassius**   To what effect?

**Casca**   Now, if I could tell you that, I couldn't look you in the eyes again! But those who understood him smiled at each other and shook their heads. Speaking for myself, it was Greek to me. I can tell you some more news, too. For pulling the decorations off Caesar's statues, Marullus and Flavius have been executed. Farewell. There was still more nonsense, if I could remember it.

**Cassius**   Will you eat with me tonight, Casca?

**Casca**   No, I am promis'd forth.

280 **Cassius**   Will you dine with me tomorrow?

**Casca**   Ay, if I be alive, and your mind hold, and your dinner
worth the eating.

**Cassius**   Good. I will expect you.

**Casca**   Do so. Farewell, both.

[*Exit* **Casca**]

285 **Brutus**   What a blunt fellow is this grown to be!
He was quick mettle when he went to school.

**Cassius**   So is he now in execution
Of any bold or noble enterprise,
However he puts on this tardy form.
290   This rudeness is a sauce to his good wit,
Which gives men stomach to digest his words
With better appetite.

**Brutus**   And so it is. For this time I will leave you.
Tomorrow, if you please to speak with me,
295   I will come home to you; or if you will,
Come home to me, and I will wait for you.

**Cassius**   I will do so: till then, think of the world.

[*Exit* **Brutus**]

Well, Brutus, thou art noble; yet I see
Thy honourable mettle may be wrought
300   From that it is dispos'd: therefore 'tis meet
That noble minds keep ever with their likes;
For who so firm that cannot be seduc'd?
Caesar doth bear me hard; but he loves Brutus.
If I were Brutus now, and he were Cassius,

**Casca**  No, I'm busy.

**Cassius**  Will you dine with me tomorrow?

**Casca**  Yes, if I'm still alive, and you haven't changed your mind, and your dinner is worth eating!

**Cassius**  Good. I'll expect you.

**Casca**  Yes, do. Goodbye to you both.

[**Casca** *leaves*]

**Brutus**  What a blunt fellow he's grown up to be! He was sharp enough when he was at school.

**Cassius**  He still is when taking part in bold or noble enterprises. This abrupt manner is something he puts on. His abrasiveness makes his shrewd remarks more palatable. Men can stomach what he says: it's more digestible and appetizing.

**Brutus**  [*smiling*] And so it is! For now, I'll leave you. Tomorrow, if you want to talk to me, I'll call on you. Or, if you wish, come to my place, and I'll be waiting for you.

**Cassius**  I'll do that. Meanwhile, think things over.

[**Brutus** *leaves*]

Well, Brutus, you are noble. But I can tell that your honorable qualities can be given a new direction. Therefore, men of noble minds should always mix with their kind. Who is so incorruptible that he can't be seduced? Caesar has a grudge against me, but he likes Brutus. If I were Brutus, and he were

305    He should not humour me. I will this night,
       In several hands, in at his windows throw,
       As if they came from several citizens,
       Writings, all tending to the great opinion
       That Rome holds of his name; wherein obscurely
310    Caesar's ambition shall be glanced at.
       And after this, let Caesar seat him sure,
       For we will shake him, or worse days endure.

                                              [*Exit*]


## Scene 3

*A street. Thunder and lightning. Enter* **Casca** *and* **Cicero**.


**Cicero**    Good even, Casca: brought you Caesar home?
       Why are you breathless? and why stare you so?

**Casca**    Are you not mov'd, when all the sway of earth
       Shakes like a thing unfirm? O Cicero,
5      I have seen tempests, when the scolding winds
       Have riv'd the knotty oaks; and I have seen
       Th' ambitious ocean swell and rage and foam,
       To be exalted with the threat'ning clouds:
       But never till tonight, never till now,
10     Did I go through a tempest dropping fire.
       Either there is a civil strife in heaven,
       Or else the world, too saucy with the gods,
       Incenses them to send destruction.

       **Cicero**    Why, saw you any thing more wonderful?

15 **Casca**    A common slave, you know him well by sight,
       Held up his left hand, which did flame and burn

Cassius, he wouldn't play his tricks on me! Tonight I'll throw notes through his open window, in different handwritings, pretending they come from various citizens, all referring to his high reputation among Romans. I'll make subtle references to Caesar's ambitions. After that, Caesar had better sit tight, because we'll undermine him, or suffer the consequences!

[*He leaves*]

## Scene 3

*A street in Rome. A storm is raging. Casca meets* **Cicero**.

**Cicero**   Good evening, Casca. Have you taken Caesar home? Why are you so breathless? So wide-eyed?

**Casca**   Aren't you upset when the entire world shakes as if it's insecure? Oh, Cicero, I've seen tempests when violent winds have split substantial oaks. I've seen the aggressive ocean swell, grow angry, and break into a foam, to join the threatening clouds on high. But never till tonight – never till now – have I ever endured a tempest featuring balls of fire. Either there's civil war in heaven, or else the world has grievously offended the gods, and provoked them into sending down destruction.

**Cicero**   Why? Did you see anything else that was strange?

**Casca**   An ordinary slave – you know him well by sight – held up his left hand, which burst into flames and burned like

Like twenty torches join'd; and yet his hand,
Not sensible of fire, remain'd unscorch'd.
Besides (I ha' not since put up my sword)
20  Against the Capitol I met a lion,
Who glazed upon me, and went surly by,
Without annoying me. And there were drawn
Upon a heap a hundred ghastly women,
Transformed with their fear, who swore they saw
25  Men, all in fire, walk up and down the streets.
And yesterday the bird of night did sit,
Even at noonday, upon the market place,
Hooting and shrieking. When these prodigies
Do so conjointly meet, let not men say,
30  'These are their reasons, they are natural';
For I believe, they are portentous things
Unto the climate that they point upon.

**Cicero**    Indeed, it is a strange-disposed time:
But men may construe things, after their fashion,
35  Clean from the purpose of the things themselves.
Comes Caesar to the Capitol tomorrow?

**Casca**    He doth; for he did bid Antonius
Send word to you he would be there tomorrow.

**Cicero**    Good night then, Casca: this disturbed sky
Is not to walk in.

40 **Casca**                        Farewell, Cicero.

[*Exit* **Cicero**]

[*Enter* **Cassius**]

**Cassius**    Who's there?

**Casca**                        A Roman.

twenty torches put together. And yet his hand wasn't burnt, as though fire couldn't harm him. Besides – I haven't sheathed my sword since – near the Capitol I met a lion that stared at me and passed unheedingly, without hurting me. And a crowd of a hundred women, all aghast, transformed with fear, swore they saw men, all on fire, walking up and down the streets. And yesterday a night bird, an owl, sat at noon in the market-place, hooting and shrieking. When all these phenomena coincide, don't let it be said, "The explanations are such-and-such; it's all perfectly natural." Because I believe they are omens with a particular purpose.

**Cicero**   Indeed, it's most peculiar weather. But men can interpret things to suit themselves, quite differently from their original meaning. Is Caesar going to the Capitol tomorrow?

**Casca**   He is. He told Antony to let you know he'd be there tomorrow.

**Cicero**   Good night, then, Casca. We shouldn't be out walking under this stormy sky.

**Casca**   Farewell, Cicero.

[**Cicero** *goes on his way home.* **Cassius** *enters*]

**Cassius**   [*sword at the ready*] Who's there?

**Casca**   A Roman.

**Cassius**                                  Casca, by your voice.

**Casca**   Your ear is good. Cassius, what night is this!

**Cassius**   A very pleasing night to honest men.

**Casca**   Who ever knew the heavens menace so?

45 **Cassius**   Those that have known the earth so full of faults.
      For my part, I have walk'd about the streets,
      Submitting me unto the perilous night,
      And, thus unbraced, Casca, as you see,
      Have bar'd my bosom to the thunder-stone;
50    And when the cross blue lightning seem'd to open
      The breast of heaven, I did present myself
      Even in the aim and very flash of it.

**Casca**   But wherefore did you so much tempt the heavens?
      It is the part of men to fear and tremble
55    When the most mighty gods by tokens send
      Such dreadful heralds to astonish us.

**Cassius**   You are dull, Casca, and those sparks of life
      That should be in a Roman you do want,
      Or else you use not. You look pale, and gaze,
60    And put on fear, and cast yourself in wonder,
      To see the strange impatience of the heavens;
      But if you would consider the true cause
      Why all these fires, why all these gliding ghosts,
      Why birds and beasts from quality and kind,
65    Why old men, fools, and children calculate,
      Why all these things change from their ordinance,
      Their natures, and pre-formed faculties,
      To monstrous quality, why, you shall find
      That heaven hath infus'd them with these spirits
70    To make them instruments of fear and warning
      Unto some monstrous state.
      Now could I, Casca, name to thee a man

**Cassius**   It sounds like Casca.

**Casca**   You've a good ear, Cassius. What a night this is!

**Cassius**   It's a very pleasant night – for honest men.

**Casca**   Whoever knew the heavens to be so menacing?

**Cassius**   Those who have realized that earth is so full of faults. Personally I've walked about the streets at the mercy of this dangerous night, with my robe unbuttoned, Casca, as you can see, baring my chest to thunderbolts. And when forked lightning seemed to tear the skies apart, I offered myself as a prime target.

**Casca**   But why did you tempt providence in this way? Men ought to fear and tremble when the most mighty gods, by means of signs, send such dreadful messengers to terrorize us.

**Cassius**   Casca, you're dull-witted. You are lacking in true Roman spirit, or else you aren't using it. You look pale, and stare, and act afraid, and work yourself up into a state of amazement, on seeing heaven in a tantrum. But if you'd analyze the real reason why there are all these fires; why all these ghosts go gliding by; why birds and beasts change their natures; why old men, idiots and children turn to prophesying, why all these things unnaturally adopt new behavior patterns, well, you'll find that heaven has made these changes to indicate its displeasure, as a warning about some abnormal state of affairs.

   Now I could name a man to you, Casca, very similar to this

Most like this dreadful night,
That thunders, lightens, opens graves, and roars
75    As doth the lion in the Capitol;
A man no mightier than thyself, or me,
In personal action, yet prodigious grown,
And fearful, as these strange eruptions are.

**Casca**    'Tis Caesar that you mean, is it not, Cassius?

80    **Cassius**    Let it be who it is: for Romans now
Have thews and limbs like to their ancestors;
But, woe the while! our fathers' minds are dead,
And we are govern'd with our mothers' spirits;
Our yoke and sufferance show us womanish.

85    **Casca**    Indeed, they say the senators tomorrow
Mean to establish Caesar as a king;
And he shall wear his crown by sea and land,
In every place, save here in Italy.

**Cassius**    I know where I will wear this dagger then;
90    Cassius from bondage will deliver Cassius:
Therein, ye gods, you make the weak most strong;
Therein, ye gods, you tyrants do defeat.
Nor stony tower, nor walls of beaten brass,
Nor airless dungeon, nor strong links of iron,
95    Can be retentive to the strength of spirit;
But life, being weary of these worldly bars
Never lacks power to dismiss itself.
If I know this, know all the world besides,
That part of tyranny that I do bear
I can shake off at pleasure.

100    **Casca**                              So can I:
So every bondman in his own hand bears
The power to cancel his captivity.

dreadful night that thunders, lightens, opens graves and roars like the lion in the Capitol. A man no mightier than yourself, or me, in terms of personal action, yet who's become awe-inspiring, and frightening, like these strange phenomena.

**Casca**  It's Caesar you mean, isn't it, Cassius?

**Cassius**  Let it be who it is. Romans today have muscles and limbs just like their ancestors. But, alas the times! Our fathers' minds are dead, and our mothers' spirits govern us. The fact that we tolerate tyranny shows we are mere women.

**Casca**  Indeed, they say that tomorrow the senators intend to make Caesar a king, and that he'll wear his crown everywhere, by sea and on land, except here in Italy.

**Cassius**  I know where I'll sheath this dagger then! [*He mimes a stabbing action at his heart*] Cassius will rescue Cassius from slavery. With this [*he grips his dagger firmly*] , you gods, you make weak men strong. With this, oh gods, you defeat tyrants. Not even towers of stone, nor brass-lined walls, nor airless dungeons, nor iron chains, can imprison the determined spirit. Because life, when it tires of these worldly bonds, never lacks the power to end itself. If I know this, then so does all the world. Any tyranny I suffer under, I can shake off at my will.

[*The thunder continues*]

**Casca**  So can I. Every slave has the power in his own hands to escape from captivity.

**Cassius**    And why should Caesar be a tyrant then?
Poor man! I know he would not be a wolf,
105    But that he sees the Romans are but sheep;
He were no lion, were not Romans hinds.
Those that with haste will make a mighty fire
Begin it with weak straws. What trash is Rome,
What rubbish, and what offal, when it serves
110    For the base matter to illuminate
So vile a thing as Caesar! But, O grief,
Where hadst thou led me? I, perhaps, speak this
Before a willing bondman; then I know
My answer must be made. But I am arm'd,
115    And dangers are to me indifferent.

**Casca**    You speak to Casca, and to such a man
That is no fleering tell-tale. Hold, my hand:
Be factious for redress of all these griefs,
And I will set this foot of mine as far
As who goes furthest.

120 **Cassius**                        There's a bargain made.
Now know you, Casca, I have mov'd already
Some certain of the noblest-minded Romans
To undergo with me an enterprise
Of honourable-dangerous consequence;
125    And I do know, by this they stay for me
In Pompey's porch: for now, this fearful night,
There is no stir or walking in the streets;
And the complexion of the element
In favour's like the work we have in hand,
130    Most bloody, fiery, and most terrible.

[*Enter* **Cinna**]

**Casca**    Stand close awhile, for here comes one in haste.

**Cassius**   So why should Caesar be a tyrant? Poor man! He's only a wolf because he sees that Romans are like sheep. He'd be no lion if Romans were not deer. To make a big fire quickly, start with feeble straws. What trash is Rome, what rubbish, and what garbage, when its only purpose is to provide the kindling to illuminate so worthless an object as Caesar! But, oh grief! [*He pretends he may have said too much*] Where have you led me? Perhaps I'm saying this to a willing slave. In that case, I know I'll have to answer for my words. But I'm prepared for that, and I scorn danger.

**Casca**   [*warmly*] You are speaking to Casca, a man who's no sneering tattletale. Here's my hand. [*He offers it to shake*] Start a movement to put right all these wrongs, and I'll go as far as anybody.

**Cassius**   [*shaking* **Casca***'s outstretched hand*] That settles it. Now, Casca, I can tell you that I've already enlisted several of the noblest-minded Romans, to undertake with me a venture involving danger, but in an honorable cause. I know they're waiting for me outside Pompey's theater, on the porch. This being such a fearful night, the streets are empty, and the sky looks just like the work we have to do – very bloody, fiery and most terrible.

[**Cinna** *enters*]

**Casca**   Stand out of sight a moment. Here's someone in a hurry.

**Cassius**   'Tis Cinna. I do know him by his gait.
   He is a friend. Cinna, where haste you so?

**Cinna**   To find out you. Who's that? Metellus Cimber?

135 **Cassius**   No, it is Casca, one incorporate
   To our attempts. Am I not stay'd for, Cinna?

**Cinna**   I am glad on 't. What a fearful night is this!
   There's two or three of us have seen strange sights.

**Cassius**   Am I not stay'd for? Tell me.

**Cinna**                                          Yes, you are.
140 O Cassius, if you could
   But win the noble Brutus to our party –

**Cassius**   Be you content. Good Cinna, take this paper,
   And look you lay it in the praetor's chair,
   Where Brutus may but find it; and throw this
145 In at his window; set this up with wax
   Upon old Brutus' statue: all this done,
   Repair to Pompey's porch, where you shall find us.
   Is Decius Brutus and Trebonius there?

**Cinna**   All but Metellus Cimber, and he's gone
150 To seek you at your house. Well, I will hie,
   And so bestow these papers as you bade me.

**Cassius**   That done, repair to Pompey's theatre.

                                          [*Exit* **Cinna**]

   Come, Casca, you and I will yet ere day
   See Brutus at his house: three parts of him
155 Is ours already, and the man entire
   Upon the next encounter yields him ours.

**Casca**   O, he sits high in all the people's hearts:
   And that which would appear offence in us

**Cassius**    It's Cinna. I can tell by his walk. He's a friend. [*To* **Cinna**] Cinna – what's the rush?

**Cinna**    To find you. [*Peering in the dark*] Who's that? Metellus Cimber?

**Cassius**    No, it's Casca, who's joined our party. Are they waiting for me, Cinna?

**Cinna**    [*taking* **Casca***'s hand*] Glad to hear it. [*To both men*] What a fearful night this is! Two or three of us have seen some strange sights!

**Cassius**    [*insisting*] Are they waiting for me? Tell me!

**Cinna**    Yes, they are. Oh, Cassius, if you could only get the noble Brutus to join our group –

**Cassius**    Don't worry. Good Cinna [*handing him a document*], take this paper and make sure you put it on the magistrate's chair, where Brutus will discover it; [*producing another*] and throw this through his open window. [ *A third*] Stick this with wax on the statue of Brutus's ancestor. When you've done all this, make your way to Pompey's porch, where you'll find us. Are Decius Brutus and Trebonius there?

**Cinna**    Everyone except Metellus Cimber, who's gone to find you at your house. Well, I'll hurry off and spread these papers as you asked me to.

**Cassius**    [*reminding him*] When you've done that, go to Pompey's theater.

[**Cinna** *goes*]

Come on, Casca. You and I will visit Brutus at his house before dawn. We've won over three parts of him already. We'll have him entirely on our side after we've spoken to him again.

**Casca**    Oh, he's very popular with the people. What would

His countenance, like richest alchemy,
160    Will change to virtue and to worthiness.

**Cassius**    Him and his worth and our great need of him
You have right well conceited. Let us go,
For it is after midnight; and ere day
We will awake him and be sure of him.

[*Exeunt*]

seem wrong if we did it will magically become right and virtuous, with his backing.

**Cassius**    Brutus's prestige, and why we badly need him, you have rightly judged. Let's go. It's after midnight, and before day comes we must wake him and make sure he's on our side.

[*They leave together*]

# Act two

## Scene 1

*Rome. Brutus's orchard. Enter* **Brutus.**

**Brutus**  What, Lucius, ho!
I cannot, by the progress of the stars,
Give guess how near to day. Lucius, I say!
I would it were my fault to sleep so soundly.
5  When, Lucius, when? Awake, I say! What, Lucius!

[*Enter* **Lucius**]

**Lucius**  Call'd you, my lord?

**Brutus**  Get me a taper in my study, Lucius:
When it is lighted, come and call me here.

**Lucius**  I will, my lord.

[*Exit*]

10  **Brutus**  It must be by his death; and for my part,
I know no personal cause to spurn at him,
But for the general. He would be crown'd:
How that might change his nature, there's the question.
It is the bright day that brings forth the adder,
15  And that craves wary walking. Crown him? – that?
And then, I grant, we put a sting in him,
That at his will he may do danger with.
Th' abuse of greatness is when it disjoins
Remorse from power; and, to speak truth of Caesar,
20  I have not known when his affections sway'd

# Act two

## Scene 1

*Rome.* **Brutus** *is in the garden of his house. Storm clouds pass across the sky.*

**Brutus**  Hey there! Lucius! There are no stars to tell how near to dawn it is. Lucius, I say! I wish I had his weakness for sound sleep. Are you coming, Lucius? Hey? Wake up, I say! Hey, Lucius!

[**Lucius** *enters sleepily*]

**Lucius**  Did you call, my lord?

**Brutus**  Put a candle in my study, Lucius. When it's lit, come and call me here.

**Lucius**  I will, my lord.

[*He goes*]

**Brutus**  [*thinking to himself*] It can only be solved by his death. For myself, I've no personal reason to clash swords with him — it's solely for the welfare of the people. He'll take the crown. The question is, will that alter his nature? Vipers hatch on sunny days — so it's always best to step carefully. Crown Caesar? [*He pauses to think this over*] That of all things? Then, surely, we'd be giving him a sting that he could use for evil purposes whenever he wished. Greatness is misused when there's no pity in the power it wields. And to be frank about Caesar, I've never known a time when his heart ruled his head.

More than his reason. But 'tis a common proof,
That lowliness is young ambition's ladder,
Whereto the climber upward turns his face;
But when he once attains the upmost round,
25  He then unto the ladder turns his back,
Looks in the clouds, scorning the base degrees
By which he did ascend. So Caesar may;
Then lest he may, prevent. And since the quarrel
Will bear no colour for the thing he is,
30  Fashion it thus: that what he is, augmented,
Would run to these and these extremities;
And therefore think him as a serpent's egg,
Which hatch'd would, as his kind, grow mischievous,
And kill him in the shell.

[*Enter* **Lucius**]

35  **Lucius**   The taper burneth in your closet, sir.
Searching the window for a flint, I found
This paper, thus seal'd up; and I am sure
It did not lie there when I went to bed.

**Brutus**   Get you to bed again; it is not day.
40  Is not tomorrow, boy, the ides of March?

**Lucius**   I know not, sir.

**Brutus**   Look in the calendar, and bring me words.

**Lucius**   I will, sir.

[*Exit*]

**Brutus**   The exhalations whizzing in the air
45  Give so much light that I may read by them.

[*Reads*]

Everyone knows that humility is the means whereby the ambitious man climbs to the top. He uses it as a ladder, and on the way up he recognizes its usefulness. But once he's reached the top step, he turns his back on the ladder, his head in the clouds, scorning the lower rungs that got him there. Caesar may do the same. In case he does, he must be stopped. And since the case against him as he is now is weak, it must be considered this way: that what he is at present, allowed to develop, would lead to such-and-such excesses. Therefore he must be thought of as a snake's egg: hatched, it would, like all its kind, grow dangerous. So he must be killed in the shell.

[**Lucius** *returns*]

**Lucius**   The candle is burning in your study, sir. Searching the window ledge for a flint to light it, I found this note, sealed like this. [*He shows* **Brutus** *one of Cassius's letters*] I'm sure it wasn't there when I went to bed.

**Brutus**   [*taking it*] Go back to bed: it's not yet day. Isn't tomorrow the ides of March, boy?

**Lucius**   I don't know, sir.

**Brutus**   Look it up in the calendar, and tell me.

**Lucius**   I will, sir.

[*He goes*]

**Brutus**   The meteors whizzing across the skies give so much light that I can read by it. [*He opens the letter and reads aloud*]

'Brutus, thou sleep'st; awake, and see thyself.
Shall Rome, etc. Speak, strike, redress!'

Brutus, thou sleep'st; awake! . . .
Such instigations have been often dropp'd
50   Where I have took them up.
'Shall Rome, etc.' Thus must I piece it out:
Shall Rome stand under one man's awe? What, Rome?
My ancestors did from the streets of Rome
The Tarquin drive, when he was call'd a king.
55   'Speak, strike, redress!' Am I entreated
To speak, and strike? O Rome, I make thee promise,
If the redress will follow, thou receivest
Thy full petition at the hand of Brutus.

[*Enter* **Lucius**]

**Lucius**    Sir, March is wasted fourteen days.

60 **Brutus**    'Tis good. Go to the gate; somebody knocks.

[*Exit* **Lucius**]

Since Cassius first did whet me against Caesar,
I have not slept.
Between the acting of a dreadful thing
And the first motion, all the interim is
65   Like a phantasma, or a hideous dream:
The genius and the mortal instruments
Are then in council; and the state of man,
Like to a little kingdom, suffers then
The nature of an insurrection.

[*Enter* **Lucius**]

Brutus, you are asleep. Wake up, and face up to yourself. Shall Rome, etc. . . . Speak out! Strike out! Reform!

[*He lowers the paper and thinks carefully, then rereads some key passages*]

"Brutus, you are asleep. Wake up!" Similar suggestions have often been dropped in places where I've picked them up. "Shall Rome, etc." I must guess the rest: Shall Rome stand in awe of just one man? Not Rome! My ancestors drove the tyrant Tarquin from the streets of Rome when he was called a king. "Speak out! Strike out! Reform!" Are they begging me to speak my mind and to take action? Oh Rome, I make you this promise: if reform will follow from my intervention, you will have the services of Brutus unreservedly.

[**Lucius** *comes back again*]

**Lucius**    Sir, it is the fifteenth of March.

[*A knock is heard*]

**Brutus**    Good. Go to the door. Someone is knocking.

[**Lucius** *leaves*]

Since Cassius first turned me against Caesar, I have not slept. The time between first thinking about a dreadful deed and doing it, is like a nightmare, or a hideous dream. The soul and the mortal body debate the issue. One feels like a small kingdom in a state of civil war.

[*Enter* **Lucius**]

70 **Lucius**    Sir, 'tis your brother Cassius,
Who doth desire to see you.

**Brutus**                                    Is he alone?

**Lucius**    No, sir, there are more with him.

**Brutus**                                    Do you know them?

**Lucius**    No, sir, their hats are pluck'd about their ears,
And half their faces buried in their cloaks,
75      That by no means I may discover them
By any mark of favour.

**Brutus**                    Let 'em enter.

[*Exit* **Lucius**]

They are the faction. O conspiracy,
Sham'st thou to show thy dangerous brow by night,
When evils are most free? O, then by day
80      Where wilt thou find a cavern dark enough
To mask thy monstrous visage? Seek none, conspiracy;
Hide it in smiles and affability:
For if thou path, thy native semblance on,
Not Erebus itself were dim enough
85      To hide thee from prevention.

[*Enter the Conspirators*, **Cassius, Casca, Decius, Cinna,
Metellus Cimber** *and* **Trebonius**]

**Cassius**    I think we are too bold upon your rest:
Good morrow, Brutus. Do we trouble you?

**Brutus**    I have been up this hour, awake all night.
Know I these men that come along with you?

90 **Cassius**    Yes, every man of them; and no man here
But honours you; and every one doth wish

**Lucius**   Sir, it's your brother-in-law Cassius at the door, and he wants to see you.

**Brutus**   Is he alone?

**Lucius**   No, sir. There are more with him.

**Brutus**   Do you know them?

**Lucius**   No, sir. Their hats are pulled over their ears, and half their faces are buried in their cloaks, so there's no way I can recognize them.

**Brutus**   Let them come in.

[**Lucius** *leaves again*]

Here are the plotters. Oh, conspiracy! Are you too ashamed to show your dangerous looks even at night, when evil comes into its own? So where in daytime will you find a cavern dark enough to hide your monstrous face? Don't even look for one, conspiracy! Hide behind smiles and affability. Because if you go about undisguised, not even the darkness of Hell's approaches could hide you from detection.

[*The conspirators enter:* **Cassius, Casca, Decius, Cinna, Metellus Cimber** *and* **Trebonius**]

**Cassius**   I think we may have called on you too early. Good morning, Brutus. Is this inconvenient?

**Brutus**   I've been up an hour  and awake all night. Do I know these men who've come along with you?

**Cassius**   Yes, every one of them. Each holds you in honor and wishes you had the same opinion of yourself that every noble

You had but that opinion of yourself
Which every noble Roman bears of you.
This is Trebonius.

**Brutus**                              He is welcome hither.

**Cassius**    This, Decius Brutus.

95 **Brutus**                                 He is welcome too.

**Cassius**    This, Casca; this, Cinna; and this, Metellus Cimber.

**Brutus**    They are all welcome.
What watchful cares do interpose themselves
Betwixt your eyes and night?

100 **Cassius**    Shall I entreat a word?

**Decius**    Here lies the east: doth not the day break here?

**Casca**    No.

**Cinna**    O, pardon, sir, it doth; and yon grey lines
That fret the clouds are messengers of day.

105 **Casca**    You shall confess that you are both deceiv'd.
Here, as I point my sword, the sun arises,
Which is a great way growing on the south,
Weighing the youthful season of the year.
Some two months hence, up higher toward the north
110 He first presents his fire; and the high east
Stands, as the Capitol, directly here.

**Brutus**    Give me your hands all over, one by one.

**Cassius**    And let us swear our resolution.

**Brutus**    No, not an oath. If not the face of men,
115 The sufferance of our souls, the time's abuse –
If these be motives weak, break off betimes,
And every man hence to his idle bed;

Roman has. [*Introducing his companions one by one*] This is Trebonius.

**Brutus**    He is welcome here.

**Cassius**    This, Decius Brutus.

**Brutus**    He's welcome, too.

**Cassius**    This, Casca. This, Cinna. And this, Metellus Cimber.

**Brutus**    They are all welcome. What is on your minds to have kept you up all night?

**Cassius**    Can I have a word with you? [*He and* **Brutus** *go to one side*]

**Decius**    [*filling in the nervous silence*] There's the east. Doesn't day break there?

**Casca**    [*blunt as ever*] No.

**Cinna**    Excuse me, sir, it does. And those gray linings around the clouds are signs of day.

**Casca**    You'll have to admit you are both wrong. Here, where I point my sword, the sun is rising, a very southerly direction, since it is still early in the year. About two months from now, it rises much higher in the north. And [*pointing*] due east is in that direction, toward the Capitol.

[**Brutus** *and* **Cassius** *finish their private discussion and join the group*]

**Brutus**    Let me shake hands with you all again, individually.

**Cassius**    And let us swear our commitment.

**Brutus**    No, not an oath. If the looks on men's faces, our soul-searching, and the evils of our time – if these are weak motives, let's break off now. Every man can go back to his lazy

71

So let high-sighted tyranny range on,
Till each man drop by lottery. But if these,
120 As I am sure they do, bear fire enough
To kindle cowards and to steel with valour
The melting spirits of women, then, countrymen,
What need we any spur but our own cause
To prick us to redress? what other bond
125 Than secret Romans, that have spoke the word,
And will not palter? and what other oath
Than honesty to honesty engag'd,
That this shall be, or we will fall for it?
Swear priests and cowards, and men cautelous,
130 Old feeble carrions, and such suffering souls
That welcome wrongs; unto bad causes swear
Such creatures as men doubt; but do not stain
The even virtue of our enterprise,
Nor th' insuppressive mettle of our spirits,
135 To think that or our cause or our performance
Did need an oath; when every drop of blood
That every Roman bears, and nobly bears,
Is guilty of a several bastardy,
If he do break the smallest particle
140 Of any promise that hath pass'd from him.

**Cassius**   But what of Cicero? Shall we sound him?
I think he will stand very strong with us.

**Casca**   Let us not leave him out.

**Cinna**                          No, by no means.

**Metellus**   O, let us have him, for his silver hairs
145 Will purchase us a good opinion,
And buy men's voices to commend our deeds.
It shall be said his judgment rul'd our hands;
Our youths and wildness shall no whit appear,
But all be buried in his gravity.

bed: tyranny, from its vantage point, can then continue to pick off its victims one by one, as though by lottery. But if these motives have enough spark about them to inspire cowards and make women brave – as I'm sure they do – then, countrymen, why do we need any incentive, other than our cause? What other bond than the fact that we are Romans, who have pledged our words, and so will not play false? What other oath than a gentleman's agreement that "this certain thing" shall happen, or we'll die for it? Priests and cowards and crafty men, old dodderers, and tormented people who enjoy deceit – they swear oaths. Men who can't be trusted are sworn into evil causes. So don't stain the purity of our scheme, nor our unconquerable will, by supposing that either our cause or our actions requires an oath. If anyone breaks his word, however slightly, then every noble drop of Roman blood he bears would be adulterated.

**Cassius**   But what of Cicero? Shall we sound him out? I think he'll stand strong with us.

**Casca**   Let us not leave him out.

**Cinna**   No, by no means.

**Metellus**   Oh, let us have him with us – his silver hairs will purchase us good opinions and buy support for what we do. People will say he influenced us. Our youth and hotheadedness will be overlooked, concealed behind his gravity.

150 **Brutus**   O, name him not; let us not break with him;
      For he will never follow any thing
      That other men begin.

   **Cassius**                      Then leave him out.

   **Casca**   Indeed he is not fit.

   **Decius**   Shall no man else be touch'd but only Caesar?

155 **Cassius**   Decius, well urg'd. I think it is not meet,
      Mark Antony, so well belov'd of Caesar,
      Should outlive Caesar: we shall find of him
      A shrewd contriver; and you know, his means,
      If he improve them, may well stretch so far
160   As to annoy us all; which to prevent,
      Let Antony and Caesar fall together.

   **Brutus**   Our course will seem too bloody, Caius Cassius,
      To cut the head off and then hack the limbs,
      Like wrath in death and envy afterwards;
165   For Antony is but a limb of Caesar.
      Let's be sacrificers, but not butchers, Caius.
      We all stand up against the spirit of Caesar,
      And in the spirit of men there is no blood.
      O, that we then could come by Caesar's spirit,
170   And not dismember Caesar! But, alas,
      Caesar must bleed for it. And, gentle friends,
      Let's kill him boldly, but not wrathfully;
      Let's carve him as a dish fit for the gods,
      Not hew him as a carcass fit for hounds.
175   And let our hearts, as subtle masters do,
      Stir up their servants to an act of rage,
      And after seem to chide 'em. This shall make
      Our purpose necessary, and not envious;
      Which so appearing to the common eyes,
180   We shall be call'd purgers, not murderers.

**Brutus**  Oh, don't ask him. Don't let him into our secret. He never follows anything that other men begin.

**Cassius**  [*anxious not to upset* **Brutus**] Then leave him out.

**Casca**  Agreed. He isn't suitable.

**Decius**  Are we going for Caesar only?

**Cassius**  A good point, Decius. I don't think it's sensible that Mark Antony, such a favorite of Caesar's, should outlive him. He's a shrewd contriver. And, you know, if he used his talents to his advantage, he might well be capable of doing us some harm. To prevent this, Antony and Caesar should die together.

**Brutus**  Our plan will seem too bloody, Caius Cassius, if we cut the head off and then proceed to hack the limbs, as if we killed in anger and afterward felt malice. Antony is only an offshoot of Caesar. We must be sacrificers, not butchers, Caius. It's Caesar's spirit we stand up against, and the spirit of men contains no blood. If only we could seize his spirit, and not dismember him! But, alas, Caesar's body must suffer. So, noble friends, let's kill him boldly, but not angrily. Let's carve him as a dish fit for the gods, not hack him like a carcass fit for dogs. And just as crafty masters provoke their servants to do certain things in anger, and later rebuke them, so our hearts should stir our passions. This will prove our scheme was necessary, not malicious, and when this is generally understood, we'll be called healers, not murderers. As for

And for Mark Antony, think not of him;
For he can do no more than Caesar's arm
When Caesar's head is off.

**Cassius**                    Yet I fear him;
For the ingrafted love he bears to Caesar –

185 **Brutus**   Alas, good Cassius, do not think of him:
If he love Caesar, all that he can do
Is to himself: take thought, and die for Caesar.
And that were much he should; for he is given
To sports, to wildness, and much company.

190 **Trebonius**   There is no fear in him; let him not die;
For he will live, and laugh at this hereafter.

[*Clock strikes*]

**Brutus**   Peace! count the clock.

**Cassius**                    The clock hath stricken three.

**Trebonius**   'Tis time to part.

**Cassius**                    But it is doubtful yet
Whether Caesar will come forth today or no;
195     For he is superstitious grown of late,
Quite from the main opinion he held once
Of fantasy, of dreams, and ceremonies.
It may be these apparent prodigies,
The unaccustom'd terror of this night,
200     And the persuasion of his augurers,
May hold him from the Capitol today.

**Decius**   Never fear that: if he be so resolv'd,
I can o'ersway him; for he loves to hear
That unicorns may be betray'd with trees,
205     And bears with glasses, elephants with holes,

Mark Antony, don't worry about him. He can do no more than Caesar's arm can, once Caesar's head is cut off.

**Cassius**   Yet I fear him. His love for Caesar is deep-rooted.

**Brutus**   Really, dear Cassius, don't give him another thought. If he loves Caesar, all the damage he can do is to himself: go into a decline and kill himself for Caesar. And he's not likely to do that. He's too fond of sports, fast living and plenty of company.

**Trebonius**   We needn't fear him. Don't let him die. He'll live to laugh about this later.

[*A clock strikes*]

**Brutus**   Hush! Count the chimes.

**Cassius**   The clock has struck three.

**Trebonius**   It's time we parted.

**Cassius**   But it's still doubtful whether Caesar will appear in public today, or not. Lately he's grown superstitious – very different from the strong views he once held about fantasy, dreams and omens. Possibly the phenomena we've been seeing lately, the unusual terrors of tonight, and the influence of his fortune-tellers will dissuade him from going to the Capitol today.

**Decius**   Don't worry about that! If that's his intention, I'll persuade him otherwise. He loves to hear how unicorns can be tricked into charging trees, bears blinded with mirrors, elephants trapped in ditches, lions caught in nets – and men

Act two    Scene 1

Lions with toils, and men with flatterers;
But when I tell him he hates flatterers,
He says he does, being then most flattered.
Let me work;
210    For I can give his humour the true bent,
And I will bring him to the Capitol.

**Cassius**    Nay, we will all of us be there to fetch him.

**Brutus**    By the eighth hour: is that the uttermost?

**Cinna**    Be that the uttermost, and fail not then.

215 **Metellus**    Caius Ligarius doth bear Caesar hard,
Who rated him for speaking well of Pompey:
I wonder none of you have thought of him.

**Brutus**    Now good Metellus, go along by him:
He loves me well, and I have given him reasons;
220    Send him but hither, and I'll fashion him.

**Cassius**    The morning comes upon 's: we'll leave you, Brutus.
And friends, disperse yourselves; but all remember
What you have said, and show yourselves true Romans.

**Brutus**    Good gentlemen, look fresh and merrily.
225    Let not our looks put on our purposes,
But bear it as our Roman actors do,
With untir'd spirits and formal constancy.
And so good morrow to you every one.

[*Exeunt all but* **Brutus**]

Boy! Lucius! Fast asleep? It is no matter;
230    Enjoy the honey-heavy dew of slumber:
Thou hast no figures nor no fantasies
Which busy care draws in the brains of men;
Therefore thou sleep'st so sound.

duped by flatterers. But when I tell him he hates flatterers, he says he does, little realizing he's being very flattered! Let me work on him. I can handle him the way we want. I'll get him to the Capitol.

**Cassius**    Indeed, we'll all of us be there to fetch him.

**Brutus**    By eight o'clock. Is that the latest?

**Cinna**    Agreed, the latest. [*To his companions*] Everyone be there.

**Metellus**    Caius Ligarius can't stand Caesar, because he angered him for speaking well of Pompey. I'm surprised none of you has thought of him.

**Brutus**    Well, good Metellus, go past his house. He likes me very much and owes me favors. Send him here, and I'll convince him.

**Cassius**    [*looking at the sky*] It's nearly morning. We'll leave you, Brutus. Friends, scatter yourselves. Let everyone remember what you have said, and act like true Romans.

**Brutus**    Gentlemen, look bright and cheerful. Don't let our faces betray our intentions. Look the way our Roman actors do: relaxed and dignified. So, good morning to you, every one.

[*The conspirators leave.* **Brutus** *calls*]

Boy! Lucius! Fast asleep? It doesn't matter. Enjoy your sweet sleep. Your brain isn't bothered with the ghosts and fantasies of worry. So you sleep soundly.

[*Enter* **Portia**]

**Portia**                                   Brutus, my lord!

**Brutus**    Portia, what mean you? Wherefore rise you now?
235  It is not for your health thus to commit
     Your weak condition to the raw cold morning.

**Portia**    Nor for yours neither. You've ungently, Brutus,
     Stole from my bed; and yesternight at supper
     You suddenly arose, and walk'd about,
240  Musing and sighing, with your arms across;
     And when I ask'd you what the matter was,
     You star'd upon me with ungentle looks.
     I urg'd you further; then you scratch'd your head,
     And too impatiently stamp'd with your foot;
245  Yet I insisted, yet you answer'd not,
     But with an angry wafture of your hand
     Gave sign for me to leave you. So I did,
     Fearing to strengthen that impatience
     Which seem'd too much enkindled, and withal
250  Hoping it was but an effect of humour,
     Which sometime hath his hour with every man.
     It will not let you eat, nor talk, nor sleep;
     And could it work so much upon your shape
     As it hath much prevail'd on your condition,
255  I should not know you Brutus. Dear my lord,
     Make me acquainted with your cause of grief.

**Brutus**    I am not well in health, and that is all.

**Portia**    Brutus is wise, and, were he not in health,
     He would embrace the means to come by it.

260 **Brutus**    Why, so I do. Good Portia, go to bed.

**Portia**    Is Brutus sick, and is it physical
     To walk unbraced and suck up the humours

[**Portia**, *his wife, enters*]

**Portia**    Brutus, my lord!

**Brutus**    [*startled to see her*] Portia, what's the matter? Why are
you up now? It's not good for your health to expose yourself to
the raw, cold morning.

**Portia**    Not is it for yours. You left your bed abruptly, Brutus.
Last night at supper, you suddenly got up and walked about,
thinking to yourself and sighing, with your arms across your
chest. And when I asked you what was the matter, you stared
at me roughly. I asked you again. Then you scratched your
head and peevishly stamped your foot. Again I insisted, but
you didn't reply. With an angry gesture, you indicated you
wanted me to go. So I did, fearing to worsen your impatience,
which was already excessive, and hoping it was just some
kind of mood, which every man suffers from at times. It won't
let you eat, or talk, or sleep. If your body were as affected as
your mind, I wouldn't recognize you, Brutus. Dearest, tell me
what's distressing you!

**Brutus**    I'm not well. That's all.

**Portia**    Brutus is sensible. If he were sick, he'd take some
medicine.

**Brutus**    Why, so I do. [*Obviously embarrassed*] Good Portia, go
back to bed.

**Portia**    Is Brutus sick, and is it healthy to walk about
unbuttoned, breathing the bad air of a damp morning? What,

Of the dank morning? What, is Brutus sick?
And will he steal out of his wholesome bed
265   To dare the vile contagion of the night,
And tempt the rheumy and unpurged air
To add unto his sickness? No, my Brutus;
You have some sick offence within your mind,
Which by the right and virtue of my place,
270   I ought to know of; and, upon my knees,
I charm you, by my once commended beauty,
By all your vows of love, and that great vow
Which did incorporate and make us one,
That you unfold to me, your self, your half,
275   Why you are heavy, and what men tonight
Have had resort to you; for here have been
Some six or seven, who did hide their faces
Even from darkness.

**Brutus**               Kneel not, gentle Portia.

**Portia**   I should not need, if you were gentle Brutus.
280   Within the bond of marriage, tell me, Brutus,
Is it excepted I should know no secrets
That appertain to you? Am I your self
But, as it were, in sort or limitation,
To keep with you at meals, comfort your bed,
285   And talk to you sometimes? Dwell I but in the suburbs
Of your good pleasure? If it be no more,
Portia is Brutus' harlot, not his wife.

**Brutus**   You are my true and honourable wife,
As dear to me as are the ruddy drops
290   That visit my sad heart.

**Portia**   If this were true, then should I know this secret.
I grant I am a woman; but withal
A woman that Lord Brutus took to wife;
I grant I am a woman; but withal

is Brutus sick? And does he sneak out of his warm bed to risk the unhealthiness of night, tempting the infectious, sunless air to add to his sickness? No, my Brutus. You have some harmful sickness in your mind which, as your wife, I ought to know about. [*She kneels to him*] Upon my knees, I entreat you, by my once-praised beauty, by all your vows of love and that most important vow of all that made us man and wife, to reveal to me, your very self, your other half, why you are so depressed, and who those men were who conferred with you tonight. Six or seven men have been here, hiding their faces even from the night.

**Brutus**    [*moved*] Do not kneel, gentle Portia.

**Portia**    I shouldn't need to, if you were gentle Brutus. Tell me, is it a condition of our marriage that I should not share your secrets? Am I one with you but, as it were, only after a fashion, with certain limitations, just to sit with you at meals, sleep with you, and talk to you occasionally? Is my place somewhere on the outer fringes of your needs? If it's no more, Portia is Brutus's mistress, not his wife.

**Brutus**    [*moved*] You are my true and honorable wife, as dear to me as the blood in my sad heart.

**Portia**    If that were the truth, then I should know this secret. I grant I am a woman, but also a woman that Lord Brutus took to wife. I grant I am a woman, but also a woman of nobility,

295     A woman well reputed, Cato's daughter.
      Think you I am no stronger than my sex,
      Being so father'd, and so husbanded?
      Tell me your counsels, I will not disclose 'em.
      I have made a strong proof of my constancy,
300     Giving myself a voluntary wound
      Here, in the thigh: can I bear that with patience,
      And not my husband's secrets?

**Brutus**                    O ye gods,
      Render me worthy of this noble wife!
      Hark, hark! one knocks. Portia, go in awhile;
305     And by and by thy bosom shall partake
      The secrets of my heart.
      All my engagements I will construe to thee,
      All the charactery of my sad brows.
      Leave me with haste.

*[Exit* **Portia**]

*[Enter* **Lucius** *and* **Ligarius**]

                   Lucius, who's that knocks?

310 **Lucius**    Here is a sick man that would speak with you.

**Brutus**    Caius Ligarius, that Metellus spake of.
      Boy, stand aside. Caius Ligarius, how?

**Ligarius**    Vouchsafe good morrow from a feeble tongue.

**Brutus**    O, what a time have you chose out, brave Caius,
315    To wear a kerchief! Would you were not sick!

**Ligarius**    I am not sick if Brutus have in hand
      Any exploit worthy the name of honour.

**Brutus**    Such an exploit have I in hand, Ligarius,
      Had you a healthful ear to hear of it.

Cato's daughter. Do you think that with such a father and such a husband I'm like any other woman? Tell me your secrets: I won't disclose them. My fortitude has been amply tested; I wounded myself here in my thigh voluntarily. Could I bear that patiently, and not my husband's secrets?

**Brutus**    Oh, heavens! Make me worthy of this noble wife!

[*There is a knock on the door*]

Listen! Listen! Someone is knocking. Portia, go in a moment. Soon your bosom will share my heart's secrets. I'll explain all my commitments to you, and the meaning of my worried looks. Go quickly.

[**Portia** *leaves*]

[**Lucius** *enters with* **Caius Ligarius**, *who is unwell*]

Lucius, who's knocking?

**Lucius**    There's a sick man here who wants to speak to you.

**Brutus**    [*recognizing the visitor*] Caius Ligarius! The man Metellus spoke of. Boy, you may go.

[**Lucius** *leaves*]

Caius Ligarius, how are you?

**Ligarius**    Accept a "good morning" from a feeble tongue.

**Brutus**    What an unfortunate time you've chosen, brave Caius, to be sick! I wish you were not.

**Ligarius**    I am not sick if Brutus has an honorable plan in hand.

**Brutus**    I have such a plan in hand, Ligarius, if only your ear was fit enough to hear about it.

320 **Ligarius**   By all the gods that Romans bow before,
   I here discard my sickness. Soul of Rome!
   Brave son, deriv'd from honourable loins!
   Thou, like an exorcist, hast conjur'd up
   My mortified spirit. Now bid me run,
325 And I will strive with things impossible,
   Yea, get the better of them. What's to do?

**Brutus**   A piece of work that will make sick men whole.

**Ligarius**   But are not some whole that we must make sick?

**Brutus**   That must we also. What it is, my Caius,
330 I shall unfold to thee, as we are going
   To whom it must be done.

**Ligarius**                     Set on your foot,
   And with a heart new-fir'd I follow you,
   To do I know not what; but it sufficeth
   That Brutus leads me on.

**Brutus**                     Follow me then.

                                    [*Exeunt*]


## Scene 2

*Caesar's house. Thunder and lightning. Enter* **Caesar** *in his night-gown.*


**Caesar**   Nor heaven nor earth have been at peace tonight:
   Thrice hath Calpurnia in her sleep cried out,
   'Help, ho! they murder Caesar!' Who's within?

**Ligarius**    [*delighted*] By all the gods that Romans worship, my sickness is cured! You are the very soul of Rome – the noble son of a distinguished father! Like a magician, you've brought my dead spirits to life. Give me my orders, and I'll tackle the impossible and make it work. What has to be done?

**Brutus**    A piece of work that will make sick men whole.

**Ligarius**    [*guessing at the plot*] But are not some whole that we must make sick?

**Brutus**    That's got to be done, too. The details, Caius, I'll explain to you on our way to this particular person.

**Ligarius**    Lead the way, and with new fire in my heart I'll follow you. What it is I have to do, I don't yet know: it's enough for me that Brutus leads me.

**Brutus**    Follow me then.

[*They depart into the stormy night*]

# Scene 2

*Rome. Caesar's house.* **Caesar** *enters in his nightgown. The storm still rages.*

**Caesar**    Neither heaven nor earth has been calm tonight. Three times Calpurnia has cried out in her sleep, "Help, there! They are murdering Caesar!" [*Calling to servant*] Who's there?

[*Enter a* **Servant**]

**Servant**    My lord?

5  **Caesar**    Go bid the priests do present sacrifice,
        And bring me their opinions of success.

**Servant**    I will, my lord.

[*Exit*]

[*Enter* **Calpurnia**]

**Calpurnia**    What mean you, Caesar? Think you to walk forth?
        You shall not stir out of your house today.

10  **Caesar**    Caesar shall forth. The things that threaten'd me
        Ne'er look'd but on my back; when they shall see
        The face of Caesar, they are vanished.

**Calpurnia**    Caesar, I never stood on ceremonies,
        Yet now they fright me. There is one within,
15      Besides the things that we have heard and seen,
        Recounts most horrid sights seen by the watch.
        A lioness hath whelped in the streets,
        And graves have yawn'd and yielded up their dead;
        Fierce fiery warriors fight upon the clouds
20      In ranks and squadrons and right form of war,
        Which drizzled blood upon the Capitol;
        The noise of battle hurtled in the air,
        Horses did neigh, and dying men did groan,
        And ghosts did shriek and squeal about the streets.
25      O Caesar, these things are beyond all use,
        And I do fear them.

**Caesar**                    What can be avoided
        Whose end is purpos'd by the mighty gods?

[*A **Servant** enters*]

**Servant**   My lord?

**Caesar**   Ask the priests to make an immediate sacrifice, and bring me the result.

**Servant**   I will, my lord.

[**Calpurnia** *enters*]

**Calpurnia**   What do you intend, Caesar? Are you thinking of going out? You shall not stir out of your house today.

**Caesar**   [*pompously*] Caesar shall go forth. Things that threaten me do so behind my back. When I turn around, they disappear.

**Calpurnia**   Caesar, I never cared about omens, but now they frighten me. Someone reports – besides the things that we have heard and seen – that the night watch saw some very horrible sights. A lioness gave birth in the street. Graves split open, revealing the corpses. Up in the clouds, fierce and fiery warriors fought in regular battle order, causing blood to drizzle on the Capitol. The noise of battle clattered in the air. Horses neighed and dying men groaned. Ghosts shrieked and squealed in the streets. Oh, Caesar, all these things are so abnormal! I fear them!

**Caesar**   What the gods have destined cannot be avoided. So

Yet Caesar shall go forth; for these predictions
Are to the world in general as to Caesar.

30 **Calpurnia**   When beggars die, there are no comets seen;
The heavens themselves blaze forth the death of princes.

**Caesar**   Cowards die many times before their deaths;
The valiant never taste of death but once.
Of all the wonders that I yet have heard,
35 It seems to me most strange that men should fear,
Seeing that death, a necessary end,
Will come when it will come.

[*Enter a* **Servant**]

What say the augurers?

**Servant**   They would not have you to stir forth today.
Plucking the entrails of an offering forth,
40 They could not find a heart within the beast.

**Caesar**   The gods do this in shame of cowardice:
Caesar should be a beast without a heart
If he should stay at home today for fear.
No, Caesar shall not. Danger knows full well
45 That Caesar is more dangerous than he.
We are two lions litter'd in one day,
And I the elder and more terrible,
And Caesar shall go forth.

**Calpurnia**                     Alas, my lord,
Your wisdom is consum'd in confidence.
50 Do not go forth today: call it my fear
That keeps you in the house, and not your own.
We'll send Mark Antony to the Senate House,
And he shall say you are not well today.
Let me upon my knee prevail in this.

Caesar shall go forth. These predictions apply as much to the world in general as to Caesar.

**Calpurnia**   When beggars die, no comets are seen. The heavens themselves proclaim the deaths of princes.

**Caesar**   Cowards die many times before their deaths; brave men die only once. Of all the wonders that I yet have heard, it seems to me most strange that men should fear death, seeing that it is inescapable. It will come when it will come.

[*A* **Servant** *enters*]

What do the fortune-tellers say?

**Servant**   They advise you against going out today. Opening up the innards of a sacrifice, they couldn't find a heart inside the beast.

**Caesar**   The gods are showing disapproval of cowardice. Caesar would be a beast without a heart if he stayed home today from fear. No, Caesar won't. Danger knows very well that Caesar is more dangerous than he is. We are like two lions born on the same day – I am the elder of the two, and the most terrible. So Caesar shall go forth.

**Calpurnia**   Alas, my lord, your confidence has overruled your common sense. Don't go out today. Say it's my fear that keeps you indoors, not your own. We'll send Mark Antony to the Senate House. He can say you aren't well today. [*Kneeling, very anxious*] On my knees, I beg you to listen to me.

55 **Caesar**    Mark Antony shall say I am not well,
And for thy humour I will stay at home.

[*Enter* **Decius**]

Here's Decius Brutus; he shall tell them so.

**Decius**    Caesar, all hail! Good morrow, worthy Caesar.
I come to fetch you to the Senate House.

60 **Caesar**    And you are come in very happy time
To bear my greeting to the senators,
And tell them that I will not come today:
Cannot is false; and that I dare not, falser;
I will not come today. Tell them so, Decius.

**Calpurnia**    Say he is sick.

65 **Caesar**                    Shall Caesar send a lie?
Have I in conquest stretch'd mine arm so far,
To be afeard to tell greybeards the truth?
Decius, go tell them Caesar will not come.

**Decius**    Most mighty Caesar, let me know some cause,
70    Lest I be laugh'd at when I tell them so.

**Caesar**    The cause is in my will: I will not come;
That is enough to satisfy the Senate.
But for your private satisfaction,
Because I love you, I will let you know:
75    Calpurnia here, my wife, stays me at home.
She dreamt tonight she saw my statue,
Which like a fountain with an hundred spouts
Did run pure blood; and many lusty Romans
Came smiling, and did bathe their hands in it.
80    And these does she apply for warnings and portents
And evils imminent; and on her knee
Hath begg'd that I will stay at home today.

**Caesar**    [*patting her head*] Mark Antony shall say I'm sick. To please you I'll stay at home.

[**Decius** *enters*]

Here's Decius Brutus. He shall tell them so.

**Decius**    [*saluting*] Caesar, all hail! Good morning, worthy Caesar. I've come to fetch you to the Senate House.

**Caesar**    You came just in time to convey my greetings to the senators, and to tell them that I will not come today. "Cannot" is untrue. "Dare not" is even falser. I *will* not come today. Tell them so, Decius.

**Calpurnia**    Say he is sick.

**Caesar**    [*rebuking her*] Shall Caesar send a lie? Have I made such extensive conquests, only to be afraid of telling old men the truth? Decius, go tell them Caesar *will* not come.

**Decius**    Most mighty Caesar, give me some reason, in case I'm laughed at when I tell them that.

**Caesar**    The reason is my will. I will not come. That should be enough to satisfy the Senate. But for your personal information, because I like you, I'll tell you this. Calpurnia here, my wife, wants me to stay at home. Last night she dreamed she saw my statue, and it was like a fountain with a hundred spouts, all running pure blood. And many noble Romans came smiling to bathe their hands in it. These she takes to be warnings and omens of imminent evils. On her knees, she has begged me to stay at home today.

**Decius**    This dream is all amiss interpreted;
It was a vision fair and fortunate:
85    Your statue spouting blood in many pipes,
In which so many smiling Romans bath'd,
Signifies that from you great Rome shall suck
Reviving blood, and that great men shall press
For tinctures, stains, relics, and cognizance.
90    This by Calpurnia's dream is signified.

**Caesar**    And this way have you well expounded it.

**Decius**    I have, when you have heard what I can say:
And know it now. The Senate have concluded
To give this day a crown to mighty Caesar.
95    If you shall send them word you will not come,
Their minds may change. Besides, it were a mock
Apt to be render'd, for some one to say,
'Break up the Senate till another time,
When Caesar's wife shall meet with better dreams.'
100    If Caesar hide himself, shall they not whisper,
'Lo, Caesar is afraid'?
Pardon me, Caesar; for my dear dear love
To your proceeding bids me tell you this,
And reason to my love is liable.

105 **Caesar**    How foolish do your fears seem now, Calpurnia!
I am ashamed I did yield to them.
Give me my robe, for I will go.

[*Enter* **Publius, Brutus, Ligarius, Metellus, Casca,
Trebonius** *and* **Cinna**]

And look where Publius is come to fetch me.

**Publius**    Good morrow, Caesar.

**Caesar**                                    Welcome, Publius.
110    What, Brutus, are you stirr'd so early too?

**Decius**   [*quick-witted*] This dream was interpreted incorrectly. It is a fair and promising vision. Your statue spouting blood through many pipes, in which so many smiling Romans bathed, signifies that great Rome regards you as its lifeblood, and that great men look to you for honors, and souvenirs to venerate. This is what Calpurnia's dream meant.

**Caesar**   [*flattered*] And this way you have rightly interpreted it.

**Decius**   [*pressing his advantage*] I have, when you have heard what I can reveal; so mark my news. The Senate has decided to offer a crown to mighty Caesar today. If you send word you will not come, their minds might change. Besides, someone might say sarcastically, "Let's suspend the Senate till another time, till Caesar's wife has better dreams." If Caesar hides himself, won't people whisper, "Oh, Caesar is afraid"? My apologies, Caesar. It's my dear, dear concern for your career that makes me speak out of turn. My love overrides my discretion.

**Caesar**   [ *to* **Calpurnia**] How foolish your fears seem now, Calpurnia! I'm ashamed I gave way to them. Give me my robe. I'll go.

[*Enter* **Brutus, Caius Ligarius, Metellus Cimber, Casca, Trebonius, Cinna** *and* **Publius**]

And look, here's Publius come to fetch me.

**Publius**   Good morning, Caesar.

**Caesar**   Welcome, Publius. What, Brutus! Are you up early too?

>Good morrow, Casca. Caius Ligarius,
>Caesar were ne'er so much your enemy
>As that same ague which hath made you lean.
>What is't a clock?

**Brutus**                              Caesar, 'tis strucken eight.

115  **Caesar**    I thank you for your pains and courtesy.

[*Enter* **Antony**]

>See! Antony, that revels long a-nights,
>Is notwithstanding up. Good morrow, Antony.

**Antony**    So to most noble Caesar.

**Caesar**                              Bid them prepare within.
I am to blame to be thus waited for.
120  Now, Cinna; now, Metellus; what, Trebonius:
I have an hour's talk in store for you;
Be near me, that I may remember you.

**Trebonius**    Caesar, I will: [*Aside*] and so near will I be,
That your best friends shall wish I had been further.

125  **Caesar**    Good friends, go in, and taste some wine with me;
And we, like friends, will straightway go together.

**Brutus**    [*Aside*] That every like is not the same, O Caesar!
The heart of Brutus yearns to think upon.

[*Exeunt*]

Good morning Casca! Caius Ligarius – Caesar was never so great an enemy of yours as that illness which has made you thin. What's the time?

**Brutus**    Caesar, eight o'clock has struck.

**Caesar**    [*excessively gracious*] Thank you for your trouble.

[**Antony** *enters*]

Look! Even Antony, the late-night reveler, is up! Good morning, Antony!

**Antony**    And to you, most noble Caesar.

**Caesar**    [*to* **Servants**] Tell them to make preparations within. [*To the visitors, with a grand humility*] I'm to blame for keeping you waiting. [*He greets each one affably*] Well now, Cinna; how now, Metellus; what, Trebonius: I have an hour's talk in store for you. Be at my side, so I can keep you in mind.

**Trebonius**    I will, Caesar. [*Aside*] And I'll be so near, that your best friends would wish I'd been further away.

**Caesar**    Good friends, go in, and taste some wine with me. Then we will go together, like friends, immediately afterwards.

**Brutus**    [*aside*] "Like" is not the same as "being." My heart grieves at the thought of it.

[*They all leave for the Capitol*]

## Scene 3

*A street near the Capitol. Enter* **Artemidorus,** *reading a paper.*

**Artemidorus**    Caesar, beware of Brutus; take heed of Cassius;
come not near Casca; have an eye to Cinna; trust not
Trebonius; mark well Metellus Cimber; Decius Brutus loves
thee not; thou hast wrong'd Caius Ligarius. There is but one
5    mind in all these men, and it is bent against Caesar. If thou
beest not immortal, look about you: security gives way to
conspiracy. The mighty gods defend thee! Thy lover,
Artemidorus.
Here will I stand till Caesar pass along,
And as a suitor will I give him this.
10    My heart laments that virtue cannot live
Out of the teeth of emulation.
If thou read this, O Caesar, thou may'st live;
If not, the Fates with traitors do contrive.

[*Exit*]

## Scene 4

*Before the house of Brutus. Enter* **Portia** *and* **Lucius.**

**Portia**    I prithee, boy, run to the Senate House.
Stay not to answer me, but get thee gone.
Why dost thou stay?

**Lucius**                    To know my errand, madam.

**Portia**    I would have had thee there and here again
5    Ere I can tell thee what thou should'st do there.

## Scene 3

*Rome. Near the Capitol.* **Artemidorus,** *a learned man, stands waiting in the street, carrying a letter which he reads aloud.*

**Artemidorus**   "Caesar: Beware of Brutus. Take heed of Cassius. Keep away from Casca. Watch Cinna. Don't trust Trebonius. Take note of Metellus Cimber. Decius Brutus doesn't like you. You have wronged Caius Ligarius. These men are all of one mind. They are against Caesar. If you are not immortal, keep your eyes open. Carelessness leads to conspiracy. May the gods defend you! Your admirer, Artemidorus." Here I'll stand till Caesar passes by. I'll give him this note as a petitioner. My heart bleeds that greatness cannot escape jealous rivalry. If you read this, Caesar, you may live. Otherwise, fate is in league with traitors.

[*He moves on*]

## Scene 4

*Outside the house of Brutus.* **Portia** *and* **Lucius** *enter.*

**Portia**   Run to the Senate House, will you, boy! Don't stop to answer me. Off you go! What's keeping you?

**Lucius**   To know my errand, madam.

**Portia**   I'd have had you there and back again, sooner than tell you why to go. Oh that I can keep a grip on myself! I wish a

O constancy, be strong upon my side;
Set a huge mountain 'tween my heart and tongue!
I have a man's mind, but a woman's might.
How hard it is for women to keep counsel!
Art thou here yet?

10 **Lucius**                    Madam, what should I do?
Run to the Capitol, and nothing else?
And so return to you, and nothing else?

**Portia**    Yes, bring me word, boy, if thy lord look well,
For he went sickly forth; and take good note
15    What Caesar doth, what suitors press to him.
Hark, boy, what noise is that?

**Lucius**    I hear none, madam.

**Portia**                    Prithee, listen well.
I heard a bustling rumour, like a fray,
And the wind brings it from the Capitol.

20 **Lucius**    Sooth, madam, I hear nothing.

[*Enter the* **Soothsayer**]

**Portia**    Come hither, fellow. Which way hast thou been?

**Soothsayer**    At mine own house, good lady.

**Portia**    What is 't a clock?

**Soothsayer**                    About the ninth hour, lady.

25 **Portia**    Is Caesar yet gone to the Capitol?

**Soothsayer**    Madam, not yet. I go to take my stand,
To see him pass on to the Capitol.

**Portia**    Thou hast some suit to Caesar, hast thou not?

**Soothsayer**    That I have, lady, if it will please Caesar

huge mountain stood between my heart and my tongue. I have the mind of a man, but the strength of a woman. How hard it is for a woman to keep a secret! [*Noticing* **Lucius** *is awaiting instructions*] Are you still here?

**Lucius**   [*bewildered*] Madam, what do you want me to do? Run to the Capitol, and nothing else? Just return to you, and nothing else?

**Portia**   Yes. Bring me word, boy, if your master looks well, because he looked ill when he left. And take good note of what Caesar does, and what petitioners crowd around him. [*She stops suddenly and listens*] Listen, boy . . . what was that noise?

**Lucius**   I didn't hear one, madam.

**Portia**   Please now, listen carefully. [*Pause. There is a silence*] I heard sounds of a disturbance like a riot, and the wind carries it from the Capitol.

**Lucius**   Honestly, madam, I can't hear anything.

[*A* **Fortune-teller** *enters*]

**Portia**   Come here, you sir. Where have you been?

**Fortune-teller**   At my own house, madam.

**Portia**   What's the time?

**Fortune-teller**   About nine, lady.

**Portia**   Has Caesar gone to the Capitol?

**Fortune-teller**   Madam, not yet. I'm going to find a place to see him pass on the way to the Capitol.

**Portia**   You have some petition for Caesar, have you not?

**Fortune-teller**   I certainly have, lady, if Caesar will do himself some good and hear me. I shall beg him to befriend himself.

30      To be so good to Caesar as to hear me:
        I shall beseech him to befriend himself.

**Portia**    Why, know'st thou any harm's intended towards him?

**Soothsayer**    None that I know will be, much that I fear may
        chance.
        Good morrow to you. Here the street is narrow.
35      The throng that follows Caesar at the heels,
        Of Senators, of praetors, common suitors,
        Will crowd a feeble man almost to death:
        I'll get me to a place more void, and there
        Speak to great Caesar as he comes along.

40 **Portia**    I must go in. Ay me, how weak a thing
        The heart of woman is! O Brutus,
        The heavens speed thee in thine enterprise!
        [*Aside*] Sure, the boy heard me. Brutus hath a suit
        That Caesar will not grant. [*Aside*] O, I grow faint.
45      Run, Lucius, and commend me to my lord;
        Say I am merry; come to me again,
        And bring me word what he doth say to thee.

                                                        [*Exeunt*]

**Portia**   [*anxious*] Why – do you know that someone intends
him harm?

**Fortune-teller**   None for certain, but a great deal might in fact
happen. Good morning to you. The street is narrow here. The
crowd of senators, officers and humble petitioners might
crowd a feeble man almost to death. I'll find a more open
space  and there speak to Caesar as he comes along.

[*He leaves*]

**Portia**   I must go in. Alas! How weak a thing is a woman's heart!
Oh, Brutus – may the gods favor your venture! [*Aside,
alarmed*] For sure, the boy heard me! [*To* **Lucius**, *trying to
explain her exclamation away*] Brutus has a request which
Caesar will not grant. [*Aside again*] Oh, I'm feeling faint. [*To*
**Lucius**] Run, Lucius, and give my good wishes to my lord. Say
I'm in good spirits. Return and bring me word what he says to
you.

[**Lucius** *leaves. After a pause,* **Portia** *returns to her house.*]

# Act three

## Scene 1

*Rome. Before the Capitol. Enter* **Caesar, Brutus, Cassius, Casca, Decius, Metellus, Trebonius, Cinna, Antony, Lepidus, Artemidorus, Publius, Popilius,** *and the* **Soothsayer.**

**Caesar**   The ides of March are come.

**Soothsayer**   Ay, Caesar, but not gone.

**Artemidorus**   Hail, Caesar! Read this schedule.

**Decius**   Trebonius doth desire you to o'er-read,
5   At your best leisure, this his humble suit.

**Artemidorus**   O Caesar, read mine first; for mine's a suit
That touches Caesar nearer. Read it, great Caesar.

**Caesar**   What touches us ourself shall be last serv'd.

**Artemidorus**   Delay not, Caesar. Read it instantly.

**Caesar**   What, is the fellow mad?

10 **Publius**                              Sirrah, give place.

**Cassius**   What, urge you your petitions in the street?
Come to the Capitol.

*[**Caesar** goes up to the Senate House, the rest following]*

**Popilius**   I wish your enterprise today may thrive.

**Cassius**   What enterprise, Popilius?

**Popilius**                              Fare you well.

*[Leaves him and joins **Caesar**]*

# Act three

## Scene 1

*The Capitol. A flourish of trumpets precedes the entry of* **Caesar**, **Brutus**, **Cassius**, **Casca**, **Decius**, **Metellus Cimber**, **Trebonius**, **Cinna**, **Antony**, **Lepidus**, **Artemidorus**, **Publius**, **Popilius**, *the* **Fortune-teller**, *and others*.

**Caesar**   [*to the* **Fortune-teller**] Well, the ides of March have come!

**Fortune-teller**   [*quietly*] Yes, Caesar. But not gone.

**Artemidorus**   Hail Caesar! Read this pamphlet!

**Decius**   [*acting quickly and handing a rival paper to* **Caesar**] Trebonius would like you to look over his humble petition, at your leisure.

**Artemidorus**   Oh, Caesar, read mine first! Mine's an appeal that's more personal to Caesar. [*Pushing his paper forward*] Read it, great Caesar!

**Caesar**   What concerns Caesar himself shall wait until the last.

**Artemidorus**   Don't delay, Caesar. Read it immediately.

**Caesar**   What, is the man mad?

**Publius**   [*pushing* **Artemidorus** *away*] Fellow, stand aside!

**Cassius**   What, are you pushing your petition here in the street? Come to the Capitol.

[**Caesar** *and the others enter the senate*]

**Popilius**   [*ambiguously*] I hope today's venture will succeed.

**Cassius**   [*startled*] What venture, Popilius?

**Popilius**   [*not to be drawn*] Goodbye to you.     105

15 **Brutus**    What said Popilius Lena?

**Cassius**    He wish'd today our enterprise might thrive.
I fear our purpose is discovered.

**Brutus**    Look how he makes to Caesar: mark him.

**Cassius**    Casca, be sudden, for we fear prevention.
20    Brutus, what shall be done? If this be known,
Cassius or Caesar never shall turn back,
For I will slay myself.

**Brutus**                    Cassius, be constant:
Popilius Lena speaks not of our purposes;
For look, he smiles, and Caesar doth not change.

25 **Cassius**    Trebonius knows his time; for look you, Brutus,
He draws Mark Antony out of the way.

[*Exeunt* **Antony** *and* **Trebonius**]

**Decius**    Where is Metellus Cimber? Let him go,
And presently prefer his suit to Caesar.

**Brutus**    He is address'd. Press near and second him.

30 **Cinna**    Casca, you are the first that rears your hand.

**Caesar**    Are we all ready? What is now amiss
That Caesar and his senate must redress?

**Metellius**    Most high, most mighty, and most puissant Caesar,
Metellus Cimber throws before thy seat
An humble heart, –

35 **Caesar**                    I must prevent thee, Cimber.
These couchings and these lowly courtesies
Might fire the blood of ordinary men,
And turn pre-ordinance and first decree
Into the law of children. Be not fond,

[**Popilius** *joins* **Caesar**, *leaving* **Cassius** *to fathom out the situation*]

**Brutus**    [*concerned*] What did Popilius Lena say?

**Cassius**    He hoped our venture will succeed today. I fear our plot has been discovered.

**Brutus**    [*keeping calm*] See how he approaches Caesar. Watch him.

**Cassius**    [*panicking*] Casca, be quick! We might be prevented. Brutus, what shall we do? If we're exposed, either Cassius or Caesar will die. I'll kill myself.

**Brutus**    [*calming him*] Cassius, keep cool. Popilius Lena isn't talking about our plot. Look, he's smiling, and Caesar's expression hasn't changed.

**Cassius**    Trebonius knows when. Look, Brutus, how he's drawing Mark Antony out of the way.

[**Antony** *and* **Trebonius** *move off*]

**Decius**    Where's Metellus Cimber? He should offer his petition to Caesar right away.

**Brutus**    He's ready. Get near him and back him up.

**Cinna**    Casca – you strike first.

**Caesar**    [*opening the proceedings*] Are we all ready? What is wrong that Caesar and his Senate must put right?

**Metellus**    Most high, most mighty and most powerful Caesar, Metellus Cimber, humble of heart, kneels before your seat [*he falls to his knees*].

**Caesar**    [*raising his hand*] I must stop you, Cimber. These bowings and scrapings might influence ordinary men and make them play about with our constitution, like children

107

40   To think that Caesar bears such rebel blood
     That will be thaw'd from the true quality
     With that which melteth fools – I mean sweet words,
     Low-crooked curtsies, and base spaniel fawning.
     Thy brother by decree is banished:
45   If thou dost bend and pray and fawn for him,
     I spurn thee like a cur out of my way.
     Know, Caesar doth not wrong, nor without cause
     Will he be satisfied.

     **Metellus**   Is there no voice more worthy than my own,
50   To sound more sweetly in great Caesar's ear
     For the repealing of my banish'd brother?

     **Brutus**   I kiss thy hand, but not in flattery, Caesar,
     Desiring thee that Publius Cimber may
     Have an immediate freedom of repeal.

     **Caesar**   What, Brutus?

55 **Cassius**                    Pardon, Caesar; Caesar, pardon:
     As low as to thy foot doth Cassius fall,
     To beg enfranchisement for Publius Cimber.

     **Caesar**   I could be well mov'd, if I were as you;
     If I could pray to move, prayers would move me;
60   But I am constant as the northern star,
     Of whose true-fix'd and resting quality
     There is no fellow in the firmament.
     The skies are painted with unnumber'd sparks,
     They are all fire, and every one doth shine;
65   But there's but one in all doth hold his place.
     So in the world: 'tis furnish'd well with men,
     And men are flesh and blood, and apprehensive;
     Yet in the number I do know but one
     That unassailable holds on his rank,
70   Unshak'd of motion; and that I am he,

playing games. Don't be so stupid as to think that Caesar has the kind of foolish heart that can be melted like those of lesser men – I mean with sweet talk, cringing bows and dog-like fawning. Your brother, Cimber, is banished according to the law. If you bow and scrape, and pray for him, I'll turn you away scornfully, like a dog. Know this: Caesar does not wrong people, nor will he be influenced except by reason.

**Metellus** [*appealing to the assembled company*] Is there no one here more worthy and acceptable to Caesar than I, to plead for the return of my banished brother?

**Brutus** [*coming forward*] I kiss your hand – but not in flattery, Caesar – asking of you that Publius Cimber's sentence may be immediately repealed.

**Caesar** [*reproaching him*] What, Brutus?

**Cassius** [*kneeling*] Your pardon, Caesar; Caesar, grant your pardon. Cassius falls to your feet to beg for Publius Cimber's reprieve.

**Caesar** I could easily concede if I were made like you. If I could get my way by asking favors, I too would be moved by prayers. But I am as unchanging as the North Star, that has no equal in the firmament for permanence and constancy. The sky is speckled with innumerable stars. They are all fiery, and each one sparkles. But only one amongst them is immovable. It's the same on earth. It is well provided with men. And men are flesh and blood, and reasoning beings. Yet of them all, I know only one who inflexibly sticks to his position, quite imperturbable, and that one is me. Let me demonstrate it a

Let me a little show it, even in this,
That I was constant Cimber should be banish'd,
And constant do remain to keep him so.

**Cinna**    O Caesar –

**Caesar**                    Hence! Wilt thou lift up Olympus?

**Decius**    Great Caesar –

75 **Caesar**                    Doth not Brutus bootless kneel?

**Casca**    Speak hands for me!

[*They stab* **Caesar**]

**Caesar**    Et tu, Brute? Then fall Caesar!

[*He dies*]

**Cinna**    Liberty! Freedom! Tyranny is dead!
Run hence, proclaim, cry it about the streets.

80 **Cassius**    Some to the common pulpits, and cry out,
'Liberty, freedom, and enfranchisement'.

**Brutus**    People and senators, be not affrighted.
Fly not; stand still; ambition's debt is paid.

**Casca**    Go to the pulpit, Brutus.

**Decius**                    And Cassius too.

85 **Brutus**    Where's Publius?

**Cinna**    Here, quite confounded with this mutiny.

**Metellus**    Stand fast together, lest some friend of Caesar's
Should chance –

little on this issue. I was firm that Cimber should be banished, and I'm firm now that he should remain so.

**Cinna**  [*moving toward* **Caesar** *as he speaks*] Oh, Caesar –

**Caesar**  Away! You might as well move Mount Olympus!

**Decius**  [*moving in on* **Caesar** *likewise*] Great Caesar –

**Caesar**  [*seeing* **Brutus** *bend his knee*] Why waste time kneeling, Brutus?

**Casca**  [*leaping on* **Caesar** *with his knife*] Deeds, not words, for me! [*The conspirators stab* **Caesar** *repeatedly*]

**Caesar**  [*as* **Brutus** *stabs*] What, you too, Brutus? [*Their eyes meet and he offers no resistance*] Then fall, Caesar!

[**Caesar** *falls to the ground, dead, blood pouring from his wounds*]

**Cinna**  [*shouting triumphantly*] Liberty! Freedom! Tyranny is dead! Run from here! Proclaim it! Cry it in the streets!

**Cassius**  Some of you go to the speakers' platforms and cry, "Liberty, freedom and democracy!"

**Brutus**  [*to the stunned onlookers*] People and senators, do not be afraid! Don't run away. Stand where you are. Ambition has got its just desserts.

**Casca**  Go to the rostrum, Brutus.

**Decius**  And Cassius, too.

**Brutus**  [*seeking* **Publius**, *the elderly senator*] Where's Publius?

**Cinna**  Here, shocked by the uproar.

**Metellus**  Stand close together, in case some friend of Caesar's should happen –

**Brutus**    Talk not of standing. Publius, good cheer;
90    There is no harm intended to your person,
Nor to no Roman else. So tell them, Publius.

**Cassius**    And leave us, Publius, lest that the people
Rushing on us, should do your age some mischief.

**Brutus**    Do so; and let no man abide this deed
95    But we the doers.

[*Enter* **Trebonius**]

**Cassius**    Where is Antony?

**Trebonius**                    Fled to his house amaz'd.
Men, wives, and children stare, cry out, and run,
As it were doomsday.

**Brutus**                    Fates, we will know your pleasures.
That we shall die, we know; 'tis but the time
100    And drawing days out, that men stand upon.

**Casca**    Why, he that cuts off twenty years of life
Cuts off so many years of fearing death.

**Brutus**    Grant that, and then is death a benefit:
So are we Caesar's friends, that have abridg'd
105    His time of fearing death. Stoop, Romans, stoop,
And let us bathe our hands in Caesar's blood
Up to the elbows, and besmear our swords:
Then walk we forth, even to the market-place,
And waving our red weapons o'er our heads,
110    Let's all cry, 'Peace, freedom, and liberty!'

**Cassius**    Stoop then, and wash. How many ages hence
Shall this our lofty scene be acted over,
In states unborn , and accents yet unknown!

**Brutus**    There's no need for that. Publius, cheer up. We don't intend to harm you or any other Roman. Tell them so, Publius. [*But* **Publius** *is too old and shocked*]

**Cassius**    And leave us, Publius, in case the people, crowding in on us, should hurt an elderly man like you.

**Brutus**    Please do – only we who did the deed must be at risk.

[**Trebonius** *returns*]

**Cassius**    Where is Antony?

**Trebonius**    He ran to his house, astounded. Men, women and children stare, cry out and run as if it's doomsday.

**Brutus**    We are in the hands of fate. We all know we shall die. It is when – and how to lengthen life – that men are concerned with.

**Casca**    Why, the man who dies twenty years before his time is spared that many years of fearing death.

**Brutus**    Accept that, and death becomes a benefit. So we are Caesar's friends, to have shortened his period of fearing death. Kneel, Romans, kneel! Let us bathe our hands in Caesar's blood, up to the elbows, and smear our swords. Then let us walk around, as far as the marketplace, and waving our blood-red weapons over our heads, let's all cry, ''Peace, freedom and liberty!''

**Cassius**    Kneel then, and wash. How many future generations will re-enact this historic scene, in countries not yet born, and in languages not yet spoken!

**Brutus**    How many times shall Caesar bleed in sport,
115    That now on Pompey's basis lies along,
No worthier than the dust!

**Cassius**                          So oft as that shall be,
So often shall the knot of us be call'd
The men that gave their country liberty.

**Decius**    What, shall we forth?

**Cassius**                          Ay, every man away.
120    Brutus shall lead, and we will grace his heels
With the most boldest and best hearts of Rome.

[*Enter a* **Servant**]

**Brutus**    Soft, who comes here? A friend of Antony's.

**Servant**    Thus, Brutus, did my master bid me kneel;
Thus did Mark Antony bid me fall down;
125    And, being prostrate, thus he bade me say:
Brutus is noble, wise, valiant, and honest;
Caesar was mighty, bold, royal, and loving:
Say I love Brutus, and I honour him;
Say I fear'd Caesar, honour'd him, and lov'd him.
130    If Brutus will vouchsafe that Antony
May safely come to him, and be resolv'd
How Caesar hath deserv'd to lie in death,
Mark Antony shall not love Caesar dead
So well as Brutus living; but will follow
135    The fortunes and affairs of noble Brutus
Through the hazards of this untrod state,
With all true faith. So says my master Antony.

**Brutus**    Thy master is a wise and valiant Roman;
I never thought him worse.
140    Tell him, so please him come unto this place,

**Brutus**    How many times will Caesar, who now lies stretched along the base of Pompey's statue, less than the dust, be made to bleed in effigy?

**Cassius**    As often as that shall be, so often shall we ringleaders be called "the men who gave their country liberty."

**Decius**    Well, shall we go now?

**Cassius**    Yes — we must all leave. Brutus shall lead the way, and we'll follow close behind him with the bravest and truest men of Rome.

[*A* **Servant** *enters, falling to his knees before* **Brutus**]

**Brutus**    One moment! Who is this? A friend of Antony's?

**Servant**    My master ordered me to kneel before you like this, Brutus. Thus did Mark Antony bid me to fall down. And, prostrate before you, he told me to say: "Brutus is noble, wise, valiant and honorable; Caesar was mighty, bold, royal and loving. Say I love and honor Brutus. Say I feared Caesar, and honored him, and loved him. If Brutus will guarantee a safe passage for Antony to come to him, and explain why Caesar deserved to be killed, then Mark Antony will not love Caesar in death as much as Brutus alive. He will faithfully align himself with the fortunes and affairs of noble Brutus through the difficult period of the new government." That's what my master, Antony, says.

**Brutus**    Your master is a wise and valiant Roman. I've never said otherwise. Tell him that if he chooses to come here, he'll

He shall be satisfied; and, by my honour,
Depart untouch'd.

**Servant**              I'll fetch him presently.

[*Exit* **Servant**]

**Brutus**    I know that we shall have him well to friend.

**Cassius**    I wish we may: but yet have I a mind
145    That fears him much; and my misgiving still
Falls shrewdly to the purpose.

[*Enter* **Antony**]

**Brutus**    But here comes Antony. Welcome, Mark Antony.

**Antony**    O mighty Caesar! dost thou lie so low?
Are all thy conquests, glories, triumphs, spoils,
150    Shrunk to this little measure? Fare thee well.
I know not, gentlemen, what you intend,
Who else must be let blood, who else is rank:
If I myself, there is no hour so fit
As Caesar's death's hour; nor no instrument
155    Of half that worth as those your swords, made rich
With the most noble blood of all this world.
I do beseech ye, if you bear me hard,
Now, whilst your purpled hands do reek and smoke,
Fulfil your pleasure. Live a thousand years,
160    I shall not find myself so apt to die:
No place will please me so, no mean of death,
As here by Caesar, and by you cut off,
The choice and master spirits of this age.

**Brutus**    O Antony, beg not your death of us.
165    Though now we must appear bloody and cruel,
As by our hands and this our present act

get a satisfactory explanation – and, on my honor, he shall leave unharmed.

**Servant**  I'll fetch him right away.

[*He leaves*]

**Brutus**  I know he'll be a good friend to us.

**Cassius**  I hope so, but part of me distrusts him. My hunches are invariably right.

[**Antony** *enters*]

**Brutus**  Here comes Antony. Welcome, Mark Antony.

**Antony**  [*looking at* **Caesar**'s *corpse*] Oh, mighty Caesar! Have you fallen so low? Are all your conquests, glories, triumphs and spoils of war shrunk to this small size? Farewell.
[*Turning to the conspirators*] I don't know, gentlemen, what you intend: who else must die, who else is ripe for bleeding. If it is I, no time is more appropriate than Caesar's hour of death. Nor is any weapon half as worthy as your swords, enriched as they are with the noblest blood of all this world. I beg you, if I am condemned, to indulge yourselves now, while your hands are reeking and steaming with blood. Were I to live a thousand years, I could not be so ready to die: no place could please me so much, no way to die, as here by Caesar, and by you struck down – the finest and the topmost men of spirit of our times.

**Brutus**  Oh, Antony, do not plead for death from us. Though we must seem bloody and cruel now, by the color of our hands and the deed we've done today – you see only our hands, and

You see we do, yet see you but our hands
And this the bleeding business they have done.
Our hearts you see not; they are pitiful;
170    And pity to the general wrong of Rome –
As fire drives out fire, so pity pity –
Hath done this deed on Caesar. For your part,
To you our swords have leaden points, Mark Antony:
Our arms in strength of malice, and our hearts
175    Of brothers' temper, do receive you in
With all kind love, good thoughts, and reverence.

**Cassius**    Your voice shall be as strong as any man's
In the disposing of new dignities.

**Brutus**    Only be patient till we have appeas'd
180    The multitude, beside themselves with fear,
And then we will deliver you the cause
Why I, that did love Caesar when I struck him,
Have thus proceeded.

**Antony**               I doubt not of your wisdom.
Let each man render me his bloody hand.
185    First, Marcus Brutus, will I shake with you;
Next Caius Cassius, do I take your hand;
Now, Decius Brutus, yours; now yours, Metellus;
Yours, Cinna; and, my valiant Casca, yours;
Though last, not least in love, yours, good Trebonius.
190    Gentlemen all – alas, what shall I say?
My credit now stands on such slippery ground,
That one of two bad ways you must conceit me,
Either a coward, or a flatterer.
That I did love thee, Caesar, O, 'tis true!
195    If then thy spirit look upon us now,
Shall it not grieve thee dearer than thy death,
To see thy Antony making his peace,
Shaking the bloody fingers of thy foes,

their bloody work. You cannot see our hearts! They are full of pity, and just as fire drives out fire, so pity drives out pity, and pity for the general wrongs in Rome has done this to Caesar. As far as you are concerned, Mark Antony, our swords are blunted. Our arms (cruel though they seem now) and our hearts (brotherly in their regard) welcome you to our midst: with kindest love, good thoughts  and due respect.

**Cassius**    You shall have an equal vote in the disposal of new honors.

**Brutus**    Just be patient till we've soothed the people, who are now beside themselves with fear. Then we'll explain why I, who loved Caesar when I struck him, did what I did.

**Antony**    I do not doubt your wisdom. Let me shake everyone by his bloody hand. First, Marcus Brutus, I will shake with you. Next, Caius Cassius, I take your hand. Now, Decius Brutus, yours. Now yours, Metellus. Yours, Cinna. And my valiant Casca, yours. And last, but not least in love, yours, good Trebonius. Gentlemen all – alas, what can I say? My reputation is on slippery ground. You'll judge me one of two bad ways. Either I'm a coward, or a flatterer. [**Antony** *turns again to* **Caesar**'s *corpse*] That I loved you, Caesar – oh, that's true. If your soul looks on us now, will it not grieve you more than your death to see Anthony making his peace, shaking the bloody hands of your enemies – most noble Caesar – in the

Most noble, in the presence of thy corse?
200    Had I as many eyes as thou hast wounds,
Weeping as fast as they stream forth thy blood,
It would become me better than to close
In terms of friendship with thine enemies.
Pardon me, Julius! Here wast thou bay'd, brave hart;
205    Here didst thou fall; and here thy hunters stand,
Sign'd in thy spoil, and crimson'd in thy lethe.
O world, thou wast the forest to this hart;
And this indeed, O world, the heart of thee.
How like a deer, strucken by many princes,
210    Dost thou here lie!

**Cassius**    Mark Antony –

**Antony**                    Pardon me, Caius Cassius:
The enemies of Caesar shall say this;
Then, in a friend, it is cold modesty.

**Cassius**    I blame you not for praising Caesar so;
215    But what compact mean you to have with us?
Will you be prick'd in number of our friends,
Or shall we on, and not depend on you?

**Antony**    Therefore I took your hands, but was indeed
Sway'd from the point by looking down on Caesar.
220    Friends am I with you all, and love you all,
Upon this hope, that you shall give me reasons
Why, and wherein, Caesar was dangerous.

**Brutus**    Or else were this a savage spectacle.
Our reasons are so full of good regard,
225    That were you, Antony, the son of Caesar,
You should be satisfied.

**Antony**                    That's all I seek;
And am moreover suitor that I may
Produce his body to the market-place,
And in the pulpit, as becomes a friend,
230    Speak in the order of his funeral.

presence of your corpse? If I had as many eyes as you have
wounds, and they all wept as copiously as you are bleeding, it
would become me better than negotiating a friendship with
your enemies. Forgive me, Julius! Here you were cornered,
like a hunted animal, a hart. Here you fell. And here your
hunters stand, splattered in the blood of your slaughter,
crimson with your lifeblood. Oh, world! You were this hart's
forest, and this man, indeed, was this world's heart. You lie
here like a deer, struck down by many princes!

**Cassius**  [*stopping him:* **Antony** *is getting dangerous*] Mark
Antony –

**Antony**  Excuse me, Caius Cassius. This is what the enemies of
Caesar will say. From a friend, therefore, it is surely
reasonable.

**Cassius**  I don't blame you for praising Caesar so. But what
relationship do you propose to have with us? Will you be
counted as one of our friends, or shall we press on and not
depend on you?

**Antony**  That was why I shook your hands – but I was distracted
by looking down on Caesar. I'm friends with you all, and I love
you all: hoping that you will give me reasons why, and in what
ways, Caesar was dangerous.

**Brutus**  This would be a barbarous sight if we could not. Our
reasons are so very sound that even if you were Caesar's son,
Antony, you would be satisfied.

**Antony**  That's all I ask – and that you will allow me to produce
his body in the marketplace, and speak at the funeral
ceremony, as becomes a friend.

**Brutus**    You shall, Mark Antony.

**Cassius**                              Brutus, a word with you.
You know not what you do. Do not consent
That Antony speak in his funeral.
Know you how much the people may be mov'd
By that which he will utter?

235 **Brutus**                              By your pardon:
I will myself into the pulpit first,
And show the reason of our Caesar's death.
What Antony shall speak, I will protest
He speaks by leave and by permission:
240    And that we are contented Caesar shall
Have all true rites and lawful ceremonies.
It shall advantage more than do us wrong.

**Cassius**    I know not what may fall; I like it not.

**Brutus**    Mark Antony, here, take you Caesar's body.
245    You shall not in your funeral speech blame us,
But speak all good you can devise of Caesar,
And say you do 't by our permission;
Else shall you not have any hand at all
About his funeral. And you shall speak
250    In the same pulpit whereto I am going,
After my speech is ended.

**Antony**                              Be it so;
I do desire no more.

**Brutus**    Prepare the body, then, and follow us.

                              [*Exeunt all except* **Antony**]

**Brutus**    You shall, Mark Antony.

**Cassius**    [*worried*] Brutus, a word with you. [*Aside*] You don't know what you're doing. Don't let Antony speak at the funeral. Don't you realize how much the people might be moved by what he says?

**Brutus**    With respect: I will go into the pulpit first and explain the reason for Caesar's death. I will announce that Antony speaks with our permission, and that we agree Caesar should have all proper rites and lawful ceremonies. It will do us more good than harm.

**Cassius**    I don't know what will happen. I don't like it.

**Brutus**    Mark Antony—here, you take Caesar's body. You must not blame us in your funeral speech, but speak all the good you can of Caesar and say you do it with our consent. Otherwise you cannot take any part at all in his funeral. And you must speak from the same pulpit that I use, and after I have spoken.

**Antony**    Agreed. I ask no more.

**Brutus**    Prepare the body, then, and follow us.

[*Everyone leaves except* **Antony**]

**Antony**    O pardon me, thou bleeding piece of earth,
255    That I am meek and gentle with these butchers.
Thou art the ruins of the noblest man
That ever lived in the tide of times.
Woe to the hand that shed this costly blood!
Over thy wounds now do I prophesy
260    (Which like dumb mouths do ope their ruby lips,
To beg the voice and utterance of my tongue),
A curse shall light upon the limbs of men;
Domestic fury and fierce civil strife
Shall cumber all the parts of Italy;
265    Blood and destruction shall be so in use,
And dreadful objects so familiar,
That mothers shall but smile when they behold
Their infants quartered with the hands of war,
All pity chok'd with custom of fell deeds;
270    And Caesar's spirit, ranging for revenge,
With Ate by his side come hot from hell,
Shall in these confines with a monarch's voice
Cry havoc and let slip the dogs of war,
That this foul deed shall smell above the earth
275    With carrion men, groaning for burial.

[*Enter a* **Servant**]

You serve Octavius Caesar, do you not?

**Servant**    I do, Mark Antony.

**Antony**    Caesar did write for him to come to Rome.

**Servant**    He did receive his letters, and is coming,
280    And bid me say to you by word of mouth –
O Caesar!

**Antony**    Thy heart is big; get thee apart and weep.
Passion, I see, is catching; for mine eyes,

**Antony**   Oh, forgive me, you bleeding piece of earth, that I'm so meek and gentle with these butchers. You are the ruins of the noblest man that ever lived in history. Woe to the hands that shed this precious blood! Over your wounds (which open their gashes like dumb mouths, to beg me speak for them) I make this prophecy: a curse shall plague men's lives; all parts of Italy will be burdened with domestic turmoil and fierce civil war; blood and destruction will be so commonplace, and dreadful deeds so familiar, that mothers will only smile when they see their infants cut to pieces by the hand of war, all pity gone, through seeing so much cruelty. And Caesar's spirit, roving in search of revenge, with the goddess of strife and discord at his side, hot from hell, shall in this country, with a kingly voice, cry havoc! and unleash the dogs of war, making this foul deed smell on earth like rotting corpses groaning to be buried.

[*Enter the* **Servant** *of Octavius Caesar*]

You serve Octavius Caesar, do you not?

**Servant**   I do, Mark Antony.

**Antony**   Caesar wrote asking him to come to Rome.

**Servant**   He received his letters, and he's coming. And he told me to say to you personally – [*The* **Servant** *sees the body of* **Caesar**] Oh, Caesar! [*He begins to sob*]

**Antony**   Your heart swells with grief; take yourself away, and weep. [*His own voice breaks a little*] Sorrow, I see, is catching.

Seeing those beads of sorrow stand in thine,
285    Began to water. Is thy master coming?

**Servant**   He lies tonight within seven leagues of Rome.

**Antony**   Post back with speed, and tell him what hath chanc'd.
Here is a mourning Rome, a dangerous Rome,
No Rome of safety for Octavius yet;
290    Hie hence and tell him so. Yet stay awhile;
Thou shalt not back till I have borne this corse
Into the market place; there shall I try,
In my oration, how the people take
The cruel issue of these bloody men;
295    According to the which thou shalt discourse
To young Octavius of the state of things.
Lend me your hand.

[*Exeunt, with* **Caesar's** *body*]

My own eyes, seeing your tears, begin to water. Is your master coming?

**Servant**    [*recovering*] He's camped about seven miles away from Rome.

**Antony**    Return as fast as you can and tell him what has happened. Rome is in mourning, and Rome is dangerous. This is not a safe Rome for Octavius yet. Go and tell him so. Yet stay a moment. You shall not return till I have carried this corpse into the marketplace. There I shall test out, in my funeral oration, how the people have responded to the cruel acts of these murderous men. The outcome will enable you to report the situation to Octavius. Lend me a hand.

[**Antony** *and the* **Servant** *exit with the body of* **Caesar**]

## Scene 2

*The Forum. Enter* **Brutus** *and* **Cassius,** *with a throng of*
**Plebeians.**

**Plebeians**   We will be satisfied: let us be satisfied.

**Brutus**   Then follow me, and give me audience, friends.
Cassius, go you into the other street,
And part the numbers.
5   Those that will hear me speak, let 'em stay here;
Those that will follow Cassius, go with him;
And public reasons shall be rendered
Of Caesar's death.

**1st Pleb**                    I will hear Brutus speak.

**2nd Pleb**   I will hear Cassius, and compare their reasons,
10   When severally we hear them rendered.

[*Exit* **Cassius,** *with some of the* **Plebeians**]

**3rd Pleb**   The noble Brutus is ascended: silence!

**Brutus**   Be patient till the last.
Romans, countrymen, and lovers, hear me for my cause, and
be silent, that you may hear. Believe me for mine honour, and
15   have respect to mine honour, that you may believe. Censure
me in your wisdom, and wake your senses, that you may the
better judge. If there be any in this assembly, any dear friend
of Caesar's, to him I say that Brutus' love to Caesar was no less
than his. If then that friend demand why Brutus rose against
20   Caesar, this is my answer: Not that I loved Caesar less, but
that I loved Rome more. Had you rather Caesar were living,
and die all slaves, than that Caesar were dead, to live all free
men? As Caesar loved me, I weep for him; as he was

## Scene 2

*Rome. The Forum.* **Brutus** *and* **Cassius,** *surrounded by Roman citizens* [**Plebeians**]*, arrive to make their statements at* **Caesar's** *funeral.*

**Plebeians**  Give us our answers! We want explanations!

**Brutus**  Then follow me, and give me a hearing, friends. Cassius, you go into the other street and divide the crowd. Those who wish to hear me speak, stay here; those who want Cassius, follow him. The reasons for Caesar's death will be explained publicly.

**1st Pleb**  I'll hear Brutus speak.

**2nd Pleb**  I'll hear Cassius. We'll hear their reasons separately and then compare them.

[**Cassius** *leaves, followed by a crowd of commoners.* **Brutus** *mounts the pulpit*]

**3rd Pleb**  The noble Brutus is in the pulpit. Silence!

**Brutus**  [*shouting above the noise*] Be patient till I've finished. Romans, fellow-countrymen and friends! Hear my case, and be silent, so you can hear! [*The hubbub dies down*] Believe me, for my honor's sake. Respect my honor, so that you may believe what I say. Judge me in your wisdom. Sharpen your wits, so that you may be the better judges. If, in this assembly, there should be any dear friend of Caesar's, to him I say that the love of Brutus was no less than his. If, then, that friend asks why Brutus rose against Caesar, this is my reply: Not that I loved Caesar less, but simply that I loved Rome more. Would you rather have Caesar alive, and all die slaves – than Caesar dead, to live all free men? Because Caesar loved me, I weep for him. As he was fortunate, I rejoice at it. As he

129

fortunate, I rejoice at it; as he was valiant, I honour him; but,
25  as he was ambitious, I slew him. There is tears, for his love;
joy, for his fortune; honour, for his valour; and death, for his
ambition. Who is here so base, that would be a bondman? If
any, speak; for him have I offended. Who is here so rude, that
would not be a Roman? If any, speak; for him have I
30  offended. Who is here so vile, that will not love his country? If
any, speak; for him have I offended. I pause for a reply.

**All**  None, Brutus, none.

**Brutus**  Then none have I offended. I have done no more to
Caesar than you shall do to Brutus. The question of his death
35  is enroll'd in the Capitol; his glory not extenuated, wherein he
was worthy; nor his offences enforc'd, for which he suffered
death.

[*Enter* **Mark Antony** *with* **Caesar's** *body*]

Here comes his body, mourned by Mark Antony, who though
he had no hand in his death, shall receive the benefit of his
40  dying, a place in the commonwealth, as which of you shall
not? With this I depart, that, as I slew my best lover for the
good of Rome, I have the same dagger for myself, when it
shall please my country to need my death.

**All**  Live, Brutus! live! live!

45  **1st Pleb**  Bring him with triumph home unto his house.

**2nd Pleb**  Give him a statue with his ancestors.

**3rd Pleb**  Let him be Caesar.

**4th Pleb**                          Caesar's better parts
Shall be crown'd in Brutus.

**1st Pleb**  We'll bring him to his house with shouts and
50  clamours.

was valiant, I honor him. But, as he was ambitious, I killed him. Tears are due for his love; joy, for his good fortune; honor, for his valor; and death for his ambition. Is there anyone here so lowly that he would be a slave? If there is, let him speak up, for I have offended him. Who among you is so uncivilized that he would choose not to be a Roman? If there's anyone, speak, for I have offended him. Who among you is so vile that he does not love his country? If anyone, speak; for I have offended him. I pause for a reply.

**All**    None, Brutus, none!

**Brutus**    Then I have offended none. I have done no more to Caesar than you might do to Brutus. The case for his death is on record in the Capitol. His achievements are not belittled, nor are his offenses, for which he was killed, stressed.

[**Mark Antony** *enters, with others bearing* **Caesar**'s *body*]

Here comes his body, mourned by Mark Antony who, though he took no part in his death, shall benefit from his dying with a position in our society – as all of you shall. With this I'll leave you. Just as I slew my best friend for the sake of Rome, I have a dagger for myself when my country decides it needs my death.

**All**    Long live, Brutus! Live! Live!

**1st Pleb**    Let's take him in triumph to his house.

**2nd Pleb**    Give him a statue like his ancestors.

**3rd Pleb**    Let Brutus be Caesar!

**4th Pleb**    We'll crown the best parts of Caesar in the person of Brutus!

**1st Pleb**    We'll take him home with shouts and cheers!

**Brutus**    My countrymen –

**2nd Pleb**                                Peace! Silence! Brutus speaks.

**1st Pleb**    Peace, ho!

**Brutus**    Good countrymen, let me depart alone,
And, for my sake, stay here with Antony.
55  Do grace to Caesar's corpse, and grace his speech
Tending to Caesar's glories, which Mark Antony,
By our permission, is allow'd to make.
I do entreat you, not a man depart,
Save I alone, till Antony have spoke.

60  **1st Pleb**    Stay, ho! and let us hear Mark Antony.

**3rd Pleb**    Let him go up into the public chair.
We'll hear him. Noble Antony, go up.

**Antony**    For Brutus' sake, I am beholding to you.

**4th Pleb**    What does he say of Brutus?

**3rd Pleb**                                He says, for Brutus' sake
65  He finds himself beholding to us all.

**4th Pleb**    'Twere best he speak no harm of Brutus here!

**1st Pleb**    This Caesar was a tyrant.

**3rd Pleb**                                Nay, that's certain.
We are blest that Rome is rid of him.

**2nd Pleb**    Peace! let us hear what Antony can say.

**Antony**    You gentle Romans –

70  **All**                                Peace, ho! let us hear him.

**Antony**    Friends, Romans, countrymen, lend me your ears;
I come to bury Caesar, not to praise him.
The evil that men do lives after them,

**Brutus**    My countrymen –

**2nd Pleb**    Quiet! Silence! Brutus is speaking.

**1st Pleb**    Quiet there!

**Brutus**    Good countrymen, let me depart alone, and for my sake, stay here with Antony. Respect Caesar's corpse, and give a fair hearing to Mark Antony's speech, which he is allowed to make, with our permission. I beg you, let no man depart except myself, till Antony has spoken.

[*He goes*]

**1st Pleb**    Stay, everyone, and let us hear Mark Antony.

**3rd Pleb**    Let him go into the pulpit. We'll hear him. Noble Antony, go up.

**Antony**    For Brutus's sake, I am obliged to you.

**4th Pleb**    [*a little hard of hearing*] What did he say about Brutus?

**3rd Pleb**    [*loudly*] He said: For Brutus's sake, he finds himself obliged to us all.

**4th Pleb**    He'd better not say anything against Brutus here!

**1st Pleb**    This Caesar was a tyrant.

**3rd Pleb**    Yes, that's for sure. Rome is best rid of him.

**2nd Pleb**    Quiet! Let's hear what Antony has to say.

**Antony**    [*over the noise*] Gentle Romans!

**All**    Quiet, everyone! Let's hear him.

**Antony**    Friends, Romans, countrymen – your attention, please! I come to bury Caesar, not to praise him! [*The noise subsides*] The evil that men do lives after them. The good is

133

The good is oft interred with their bones;
75 So let it be with Caesar. The noble Brutus
Hath told you Caesar was ambitious.
If it were so, it was a grievous fault,
And grievously hath Caesar answer'd it.
Here, under the leave of Brutus and the rest,
80 – For Brutus is an honourable man;
So are they all, all honourable men –
Come I to speak in Caesar's funeral.
He was my friend, faithful and just to me;
But Brutus says he was ambitious,
85 And Brutus is an honourable man.
He hath brought many captives home to Rome,
Whose ransom did the general coffers fill:
Did this in Caesar seem ambitious?
When that the poor have cried, Caesar hath wept;
90 Ambition should be made of sterner stuff:
Yet Brutus says he was ambitious,
And Brutus is an honourable man.
You all did see that on the Lupercal
I thrice presented him a kingly crown,
95 Which he did thrice refuse. Was this ambition?
Yet Brutus says he was ambitious,
And sure he is an honourable man.
I speak not to disprove what Brutus spoke,
But here I am to speak what I do know.
100 You all did love him once, not without cause;
What cause withholds you then to mourn for him?
O judgment, thou art fled to brutish beasts,
And men have lost their reason. Bear with me.
My heart is in the coffin there with Caesar,
105 And I must pause till it come back to me.

**1st Pleb**   Methinks there is much reason in his sayings.

**2nd Pleb**   If thou consider rightly of the matter,
Caesar has had great wrong.

often buried with their bones. So let it be with Caesar. The noble Brutus has told you that Caesar was ambitious. If he was, it was a grievous fault, and Caesar has grievously suffered for it. I come here, by permission of Brutus and the others – for Brutus is an honorable man; so are they all, all honorable men – to speak at Caesar's funeral. He was my friend, faithful and just to me. But Brutus says he was ambitious – and Brutus is an honorable man. He has brought many prisoners back home to Rome, whose ransoms filled the Treasury. Did this seem ambitious of Caesar? When the poor have cried, Caesar has wept in sympathy. Ambition should be made of sterner stuff! Yet Brutus says he was ambitious – and Brutus is an honorable man. You all saw that on the Feast of Lupercal I presented him a kingly crown, three times: three times he turned it down. Was this ambition? Yet Brutus says he was ambitious – and, for sure, he is an honorable man. I don't speak to dispute what Brutus said; I'm simply here to say just what I know. You all loved him once, and not without reason. What reason therefore stops you mourning him? Oh, Reason, you have fled to animals, and men have lost their feelings! [*His voice cracks with emotion*] Bear with me. My heart is in the coffin there, with Caesar. I must pause till it returns to me.

**1st Pleb**   I think there's a lot of sense in what he says.

**2nd Pleb**   If you think about it properly, Caesar has been greatly wronged.

**3rd Pleb**                            Has he, masters?
I fear there will a worse come in his place.

110  **4th Pleb**   Mark'd ye his words? He would not take the crown;
Therefore 'tis certain he was not ambitious.

**1st Pleb**   If it be found so, some will dear abide it.

**2nd Pleb**   Poor soul! His eyes are red as fire with weeping.

**3rd Pleb**   There's not a nobler man in Rome than Antony.

115  **4th Pleb**   Now mark him; he begins again to speak.

**Antony**   But yesterday the word of Caesar might
Have stood against the world; now lies he there,
And none so poor to do him reverence.
O masters! if I were dispos'd to stir
120  Your hearts and minds to mutiny and rage,
I should do Brutus wrong, and Cassius wrong,
Who, you all know, are honourable men.
I will not do them wrong; I rather choose
To wrong the dead, to wrong myself and you,
125  Than I will wrong such honourable men.
But here's a parchment with the seal of Caesar;
I found it in his closet; 'tis his will.
Let but the commons hear this testament,
Which, pardon me, I do not mean to read,
130  And they would go and kiss dead Caesar's wounds,
And dip their napkins in his sacred blood,
Yea, beg a hair of him for memory,
And, dying, mention it within their wills,
Bequeathing it as a rich legacy
135  Unto their issue.

**4th Pleb**   We'll hear the will. Read it, Mark Antony.

**All**   The will, the will! We will hear Caesar's will!

**3rd Pleb**    Has he, friends? I fear the change is for the worse!

**4th Pleb**    Did you note his words? "He wouldn't take the crown." That proves he wasn't ambitious!

**1st Pleb**    If that's so, some will pay dearly for it!

**2nd Pleb**    Poor soul! His eyes are red as fire from weeping!

**3rd Pleb**    There isn't a nobler man in Rome than Antony!

**4th Pleb**    Listen to him. He's starting to speak again.

**Antony**    Only yesterday, the word of Caesar could have taken on the world. Now he lies here, and the humblest of men is too lofty to do him reverence. Oh, gentlemen! If I were inclined to stir your hearts and minds to riots and demonstrations, I would be doing Brutus wrong  and Cassius wrong – and they, as you know, are honorable men. I will not do them wrong. I prefer to wrong the dead, to wrong myself and you, than wrong such honorable men. [*He produces a roll of legal parchment*] But here's a document, with Caesar's seal on it. I found it in his bedroom. It's his will. If the people were to hear his testament – which, please excuse me, I don't intend to read – they would go and kiss dead Caesar's wounds, and dip their handkerchiefs in his sacred blood. Yes – they'd beg one of his hairs as a souvenir, and when they died, they'd include it in their wills, bequeathing it as a rich legacy to their heirs.

**4th Pleb**    We want to hear the will! Read it, Mark Antony!

**All**    The will! The will! We'll hear Caesar's will!

**Antony**    Have patience, gentle friends; I must not read it.
It is not meet you know how Caesar lov'd you.
140    You are not wood, you are not stones, but men;
And being men, hearing the will of Caesar,
It will inflame you, it will make you mad.
'Tis good you know not that you are his heirs;
For if you should, O, what would come of it?

145    **4th Pleb**    Read the will! We'll hear it, Antony!
You shall read us the will, Caesar's will!

**Antony**    Will you be patient? Will you stay awile?
I have o'ershot myself to tell you of it.
I fear I wrong the honourable men
150    Whose daggers have stabb'd Caesar; I do fear it.

**4th Pleb**    They were traitors. Honourable men!

**All**    The will! – The testament!

**2nd Pleb**    They were villains, murderers! The will! Read the will!

155    **Antony**    You will compel me then to read the will?
Then make a ring about the corpse of Caesar,
And let me show you him that made the will.
Shall I descend? and will you give me leave?

**All**    Come down.

160    **2nd Pleb**    Descend.

[**Antony** *comes down*]

**3rd Pleb**    You shall have leave.

**4th Pleb**    A ring; stand round.

**1st Pleb**    Stand from the hearse! stand from the body!

**2nd Pleb**    Room for Antony, most noble Antony!

**Antony**   Have patience, gentle friends. I must not read it. It's better that you do not know how Caesar loved you. You aren't made of wood, you aren't stones: you are men! And being men, hearing Caesar's will, will incense you. It will infuriate you. It's a good thing you don't know you are his heirs. If you did, oh, what might be the outcome?

**4th Pleb**   Read the will! We'll hear it, Antony! You must read us the will, Caesar's will!

**Antony**   Won't you be patient? Won't you wait a little? I've overstepped the mark to mention it to you. I fear that I wrong the honorable men whose daggers have stabbed Caesar. I really fear it.

**4th Pleb**   They were traitors! [*Scornfully*] Honorable men!

**All**   The will! The testament!

**2nd Pleb**   They were villains! Murderers! The will! Read the will!

**Antony**   You will compel me to read the will, then? [*The crowd roars its approval*] Then make a ring around Caesar's corpse, and let me show you the man who made the will. May I come down? [*All politeness*] Will you give me permission?

**All**   Come down!

**2nd Pleb**   Descend!

[**Antony** *comes down to ground level*]

**3rd Pleb**   You have permission.

**4th Pleb**   In a ring! Stand around!

**1st Pleb**   Stand away from the hearse! Keep clear of the body!

**2nd Pleb**   Make room for Antony, most noble Antony!

165 **Antony**    Nay, press not so upon me; stand far off.

**All**    Stand back! Room! Bear back!

**Antony**    If you have tears, prepare to shed them now.
You all do know this mantle. I remember
The first time ever Caesar put it on;
170 'Twas on a summer's evening in his tent,
That day he overcame the Nervii.
Look, in this place ran Cassius' dagger through:
See what a rent the envious Casca made:
Through this the well-beloved Brutus stabb'd;
175 And as he pluck'd his cursed steel away,
Mark how the blood of Caesar follow'd it,
As rushing out of doors, to be resolv'd
If Brutus so unkindly knock'd or no;
For Brutus, as you know, was Caesar's angel.
180 Judge, O you gods, how dearly Caesar lov'd him.
This was the most unkindest cut of all;
For when the noble Caesar saw him stab,
Ingratitude, more strong than traitors' arms,
Quite vanquish'd him: then burst his mighty heart;
185 And in his mantle muffling up his face,
Even at the base of Pompey's statue
(Which all the while ran blood) great Caesar fell.
O, what a fall was there, my countrymen!
Then I, and you, and all of us fell down,
190 Whilst bloody treason flourish'd over us.
O, now you weep, and I perceive you feel
The dint of pity. These are gracious drops.
Kind souls, what weep you when you but behold
Our Caesar's vesture wounded? Look you here!
195 Here is himself, marr'd, as you see, with traitors.

**1st Pleb**    O piteous spectacle!

**2nd Pleb**    O noble Caesar!

**Antony**   No, don't crowd me! Stand farther off.

**All**   Stand back! Give him room! Get back!

**Antony**   If you have any tears, prepare to shed them now. [*He holds up* **Caesar***'s cloak*] You all know this garment. I remember the first time Caesar ever wore it. It was on a summer's evening, in his tent, the very day he defeated the Nervii tribe in the Gallic Wars. Look! [*He points dramatically to rips in the torn and bloody piece of clothing*] This is where Cassius's dagger went through. See how big a tear the spiteful Casca made! Through this, the much-loved Brutus stabbed, and as he drew his cursed blade out, notice how the blood of Caesar followed it, as if it were rushing out of doors, to see whether it was Brutus who was knocking so unnaturally, or not. Because Brutus, as you know, was Caesar's darling. Judge, oh gods, how dearly Caesar loved him! This was the cruelest cut of all. When the noble Caesar saw him stab, the ingratitude of it – worse than the traitorous betrayal – quite overcame him. His mighty heart broke then. And with his cloak muffling his face, great Caesar fell, here, at the base of Pompey's statue, which all this time ran with blood. Oh, what a fall that was, my countrymen! Then I, and you, and all of us fell down, while bloody treason rampaged over us. [*The crowd is now in tears*] Oh, now you are crying! And I detect a touch of pity. These are indeed gracious tears. Kind souls, are you weeping at the simple sight of Caesar's wounded garment? [*He pulls the covering off* **Caesar***'s corpse*] Look here! Here's the man himself, disfigured, as you see, by traitors!

[*The crowd looks at the blood-covered body in horror and dismay*]

**1st Pleb**   Oh, what a piteous spectacle!

**2nd Pleb**   Oh, noble Caesar!

**3rd Pleb**    O woeful day!

**4th Pleb**    O traitors! villains!

200 **1st Pleb**    O most bloody sight!

**2nd Pleb**    We will be revenged.

**All**    Revenge! About! Seek! Burn! Fire! Kill! Slay!
Let not a traitor live.

**Antony**    Stay, countrymen.

205 **1st Pleb**    Peace there! Hear the noble Antony.

**2nd Pleb**    We'll hear him, we'll follow him, we'll die with him.

**Antony**    Good friends, sweet friends, let me not stir you up
To such a sudden flood of mutiny.
They that have done this deed are honourable.
210    What private griefs they have, alas, I know not,
That made them do it. They are wise and honourable,
And will, no doubt, with reasons answer you.
I come not, friends, to steal away your hearts.
I am no orator, as Brutus is,
215    But, as you know me all, a plain blunt man,
That love my friend; and that they know full well
That gave me public leave to speak of him.
For I have neither wit, nor words, nor worth,
Action, nor utterance, nor the power of speech
220    To stir men's blood; I only speak right on.
I tell you that which you yourselves do know,
Show you sweet Caesar's wounds, poor poor dumb mouths,
And bid them speak for me. But were I Brutus,
And Brutus Antony, there were an Antony
225    Would ruffle up your spirits, and put a tongue
In every wound of Caesar that should move
The stones of Rome to rise and mutiny.

**All**    We'll mutiny.

**3rd Pleb**    Oh woeful day!

**4th Pleb**    Oh, traitors! Villains!

**1st Pleb**    Oh, such a bloody sight!

**2nd Pleb**    We'll be revenged!

**All**    Revenge! Let's go! Seek them out! Burn! Fire! Kill! Slay!
Let not a single traitor live.

**Antony**    [*shouting*] Hold on, countrymen!

**1st Pleb**    Quiet there! Hear the noble Antony!

**2nd Pleb**    We'll hear him! We'll follow him! We'll die with him!

**Antony**    Good friends, sweet friends, don't let me incite you to
such a sudden rioting! Those who did this deed are
honorable. Alas, I don't know what private grievances they
have, that made them do it. They are wise and honorable,
and they will, no doubt, give you their explanations. I'm not
here, friends, to steal your hearts away. I'm no orator, as
Brutus is. As you all know, I'm a plain, blunt man, who loved
his friend. And those who gave me official permission to
speak of him know that full well. I have neither the intellect,
nor the fluency, nor the authority, the gestures, the delivery,
nor the persuasiveness to rouse men's blood. I just speak right
out. I tell you what you already know. I show you sweet
Caesar's wounds – those poor, poor, dumb mouths – and ask
them to speak for me. But if I were Brutus, and Brutus were
Antony, then there would be an Antony who'd stir your hearts,
and give every wound of Caesar a tongue that would move
the very stones of Rome to rise and riot!

**All**    We'll riot!

**1st Pleb**          We'll burn the house of Brutus.

230 **3rd Pleb**   Away then! Come, seek the conspirators.

**Antony**   Yet hear me, countrymen. Yet hear me speak.

**All**   Peace, ho! Hear Antony, most noble Antony.

**Antony**   Why, friends, you go to do you know not what.
Wherein hath Caesar thus deserv'd your loves?
235   Alas! you know not: I must tell you then.
You have forgot the will I told you of.

**All**   Most true. The will! Let's stay and hear the will.

**Antony**   Here is the will, and under Caesar's seal.
To every Roman citizen he gives,
240   To every several man, seventy-five drachmas.

**2nd Pleb**   Most noble Caesar! We'll revenge his death.

**3rd Pleb**   O royal Caesar!

**Antony**   Hear me with patience.

**All**   Peace, ho!

245 **Antony**   Moreover, he hath left you all his walks,
His private arbours, and new-planted orchards,
On this side Tiber; he hath left them you,
And to your heirs for ever: common pleasures,
To walk abroad and recreate yourselves.
250   Here was a Caesar! when comes such another?

**1st Pleb**   Never, never! Come, away, away!
We'll burn his body in the holy place,
And with the brands fire the traitors' houses.
Take up the body.

255 **2nd Pleb**   Go fetch fire.

**3rd Pleb**   Pluck down benches.

**1st Pleb**    We'll burn Brutus's house!

**3rd Pleb**    Let's go, then. Come on, let's find the conspirators.

**Antony**    Countrymen, listen to me. Listen to me!

**All**    Quiet there! Let's hear Antony. Most noble Antony!

**Antony**    Why, friends, you don't know what you're up to!
Why has Caesar so deserved your love? Alas, you don't know.
I'll have to tell you, then. You have forgotten the will I
mentioned.

**All**    Very true. The will! Let's stay and hear the will!

**Antony**    [*producing the document from his toga*] Here is the
will, with Caesar's personal seal. [*Reading*] To every Roman
citizen, to every individual man, he gives the sum of seventy-
five drachmas.

**2nd Pleb**    Most noble Caesar! We'll revenge his death!

**3rd Pleb**    Oh, royal Caesar!

**Antony**    Hear me patiently!

**All**    Quiet there!

**Antony**    In addition, he has left you all his walks, his private
arbors, his newly planted orchards, on this side of the Tiber.
He has left them to you  and to your heirs, forever. Public parks
— to walk around in and enjoy yourselves. That was a Caesar!
When shall we ever see his like?

**1st Pleb**    Never, never! Come on – let's go, go! We'll burn his
body in the holy place  and set fire to the traitors' houses with
the burning sticks. Lift up the body.

**2nd Pleb**    Go and get a light.

**3rd Pleb**    Pull down benches.

**4th Pleb**    Pluck down forms, windows, any thing.

[*Exeunt* **Plebeians** *with the body*]

**Antony**    Now let it work. Mischief, thou art afoot,
Take thou what course thou wilt! How now, fellow?

[*Enter a* **Servant**]

260 **Servant**    Sir, Octavius is already come to Rome.

**Antony**    Where is he?

**Servant**    He and Lepidus are at Caesar's house.

**Antony**    And thither will I straight to visit him.
He comes upon a wish. Fortune is merry,
265    And in this mood will give us any thing.

**Servant**    I heard him say Brutus and Cassius
Are rid like madmen through the gates of Rome.

**Antony**    Belike they had some notice of the people,
How I had mov'd them. Bring me to Octavius.

[*Exeunt*]

## Scene 3

*A street. Enter* **Cinna** *the poet, and after him the* **Plebeians.**

**Cinna**    I dreamt tonight that I did feast with Caesar,
And things unlucky charge my fantasy.
I have no will to wander forth of doors,
Yet something leads me forth.

**4th Pleb**    Pull down seats, shutters, anything!

[*The crowd disperses, taking* **Caesar**'s *body*]

**Antony**    Now things can take their course. Trouble's brewing. Let whatever happens, happen. [*To* **Servant**, *who has just arrived*] Yes, fellow?

**Servant**    Sir, Octavius has arrived in Rome.

**Antony**    Where is he?

**Servant**    He and Lepidus are at Caesar's house.

**Antony**    And I'll go straight there to visit him. He comes just as I'd wished. Fortune smiles, and in this mood will grant us anything.

**Servant**    I heard him say Brutus and Cassius are riding like madmen through Rome's gates.

**Antony**    Probably they've heard rumors of how I've influenced the people. Take me to Octavius.

[*They leave*]


# Scene 3

*A street in Rome.* **Cinna** *the poet (not* **Cinna** *the conspirator) is being followed by a mob.*


**Cinna**    Last night I dreamed I dined with Caesar. What has happened preys on my imagination. I have no wish to leave the house, yet something tempts me out.

5 **1st Pleb**    What is your name?

**2nd Pleb**    Whither are you going?

**3rd Pleb**    Where do you dwell?

**4th Pleb**    Are you a married man or a bachelor?

**2nd Pleb**    Answer every man directly.

10 **1st Pleb**    Ay, and briefly.

**4th Pleb**    Ay, and wisely.

**3rd Pleb**    Ay, and truly, you were best.

**Cinna**    What is my name? Whither am I going? Where do I dwell? Am I a married man or a bachelor? Then, to answer
15    every man directly and briefly, wisely and truly: wisely I say, I am a bachelor.

**2nd Pleb**    That's as much as to say they are fools that marry. You'll bear me a bang for that, I fear. Proceed, directly.

**Cinna**    Directly, I am going to Caesar's funeral.

20 **1st Pleb**    As a friend or an enemy?

**Cinna**    As a friend.

**2nd Pleb**    The matter is answered directly.

**4th Pleb**    For your dwelling, briefly.

**Cinna**    Briefly, I dwell by the Capitol.

25 **3rd Pleb**    Your name, sir, truly.

**Cinna**    Truly, my name is Cinna.

**1st Pleb**    Tear him to pieces! He's a conspirator.

**Cinna**    I am Cinna the poet, I am Cinna the poet.

**4th Pleb**    Tear him for his bad verses, tear him for his bad
30    verses.

148

**1st Pleb**    What's your name?

**2nd Pleb**    Where are you going?

**3rd Pleb**    Where do you live?

**4th Pleb**    Are you a married man or single?

**2nd Pleb**    Answer everyone bluntly.

**1st Pleb**    Yes, and briefly.

**4th Pleb**    Yes, and sensibly.

**3rd Pleb**    Yes, frankly, you'd better!

**Cinna**    What's my name? Where am I going? Where do I live? Am I married or single? Well, to answer every man directly and briefly, sensibly and frankly: to be sensible, I'm a bachelor.

**2nd Pleb**    That's like saying only fools marry. I'm going to thump you for that, I'm afraid. But proceed – bluntly.

**Cinna**    Bluntly – I'm going to Caesar's funeral.

**1st Pleb**    As a friend or enemy?

**Cinna**    As a friend.

**2nd Pleb**    That's a blunt answer.

**4th Pleb**    Your address, briefly?

**Cinna**    Briefly, I live near the Capitol.

**3rd Pleb**    Your name, sir, truthfully.

**Cinna**    Truly, my name is Cinna.

**1st Pleb**    Tear him apart! He's a conspirator!

**Cinna**    I am Cinna the poet. Cinna the poet!

**4th Pleb**    Tear him apart for his bad verses. Tear him apart for his bad verses!

149

**Cinna**    I am not Cinna the conspirator.

**1st Pleb**    It is no matter, his name's Cinna; pluck but his name out of his heart, and turn him going.

**3rd Pleb**    Tear him, tear him! Come, brands, ho! firebrands!
35    To Brutus', to Cassius'; burn all! Some to Decius' house, and some to Casca's; some to Ligarius'. Away! go!

[*Exeunt all the* **Plebeians,** *dragging off* **Cinna**]

**Cinna**  [*very anxious now*] I am not Cinna the conspirator.

**1st Pleb**  That doesn't matter. His name's Cinna. Let's just tear
his name out of his heart  and set the rest of him free.

**3rd Pleb**  Tear him! Tear him! [*The gang descend on* **Cinna** *the
poet  and drag him off to his fate*] Come on, some sticks!
Torches! Some go to Brutus's house, some to Cassius's. Burn
everything! Some to Decius's house, and some to Casca's,
some to Ligarius's. Away with you! Go!

[*They leave in riotous manner*]

# Act four

## Scene 1

*Antony's house. Enter* **Antony, Octavius** *and* **Lepidus.**

**Antony**   These many then shall die; their names are prick'd.

**Octavius**   Your brother too must die; consent you, Lepidus?

**Lepidus**   I do consent –

**Octavius**                         Prick him down, Antony.

**Lepidus**   Upon condition Publius shall not live,
5   Who is your sister's son, Mark Antony.

**Antony**   He shall not live. Look, with a spot I damn him.
  But Lepidus, go you to Caesar's house;
  Fetch the will hither, and we shall determine
  How to cut off some charge in legacies.

10 **Lepidus**   What, shall I find you here?

**Octavius**   Or here or at the Capitol.

                                    [*Exit* **Lepidus**]

**Antony**   This is a slight unmeritable man,
  Meet to be sent on errands. Is it fit,
  The three-fold world divided, he should stand
  One of the three to share it?

15 **Octavius**                         So you thought him,
  And took his voice who should be prick'd to die
  In our black sentence and proscription.

# Act four

## Scene 1

*Rome. A room in* **Antony**'s *house.* **Antony, Octavius** *and* **Lepidus** *are sorting out the aftermath of rebellion.*

**Antony**  These men, then, shall die. [*He hands over a list*] I've marked their names.

**Octavius**  Your brother, too, must die. Do your agree, Lepidus?

**Lepidus**  I agree —

**Octavius**  Mark his name, Antony.

**Lepidus**  — provided Publius dies too; that is, your sister's son, Mark Antony.

**Antony**  He shall not live. Look. [*He makes a mark on the list*] With a check, I condemn him. Lepidus — go to Caesar's house. Bring the will here. We'll decide how we can save something on the legacies.

**Lepidus**  Will you still be here?

**Octavius**  Either here or at the Capitol.

[**Lepidus** *leaves*]

**Antony**  [*looking after him  scornfully*] He's an insignificant nobody of a man; running errands suits him. Do you think it's right that with our dominions divided into three parts, he should be one of the three to have a share?

**Octavius**  You thought so once  and used his vote to decide who should be included on our death list.

**Antony**    Octavius, I have seen more days than you:
And though we lay these honours on this man,
20    To ease ourselves of divers sland'rous loads,
He shall but bear them as the ass bears gold,
To groan and sweat under the business,
Either led or driven, as we point the way;
And having brought our treasure where we will,
25    Then take we down his load, and turn him off,
Like to the empty ass, to shake his ears,
And graze in commons.

**Octavius**                    You may do your will;
But he's a tried and valiant soldier.

**Antony**    So is my horse, Octavius, and for that
30    I do appoint him store of provender:
It is a creature that I teach to fight,
To wind, to stop, to run directly on,
His corporal motion govern'd by my spirit.
And, in some taste, is Lepidus but so:
35    He must be taught, and train'd, and bid go forth:
A barren-spirited fellow; one that feeds
On objects, arts, and imitations,
Which, out of use and stal'd by other men,
Begin his fashion. Do not talk of him
40    But as a property. And now, Octavius,
Listen great things: Brutus and Cassius
Are levying powers: we must straight make head.
Therefore let our alliance be combin'd,
Our best friends made, our means stretch'd;
45    And let us presently go sit in council,
How covert matters may be best disclos'd,
And open perils surest answered.

**Octavius**    Let us do so: for we are at the stake,
And bay'd about with many enemies;

**Antony**   Octavius, I am older than you are. We give this man high office to take the blame for us when what we do is unpopular. He'll carry this burden for us as an ass carries gold: groaning and sweating with the strain, being led or driven forward according to our directions. When we've got our treasure where we want it, we'll remove the load, turn him loose, let him shake his ears like an ass set free, and graze him on the village commonland.

**Octavius**   As you wish. But he's an experienced and valiant soldier.

**Antony**   So is my horse, Octavius. That's why I feed him. It's a creature that I teach to fight, to turn, to stop, to run directly ahead, his whole body subject to my orders. To some extent, Lepidus is the same. He must be taught, and trained, and told to go places: an uninspired fellow, who has a taste for curiosities, the creative arts and works of the imagination – things which he gets to like when they are out of date and popularized by other men. Don't talk of him except as a convenient tool. And now, Octavius, to important matters. Brutus and Cassius are raising armies. We must build up our forces. So let's combine as allies, make alliances with our friends, stretch our resources to their fullest, and then immediately hold a council to decide how hidden dangers can be brought to light and open threats best answered.

**Octavius**   Let's do that, for we are surrounded by many

50   And some that smile have in their hearts, I fear,
     Millions of mischiefs.

                                                    [*Exeunt*]

## Scene 2

*Camp near Sardis. Before Brutus's tent. Drum. Enter* **Brutus,**
**Lucilius** *and the soldiers.* **Titinius** *and* **Pindarus** *meet them.*

**Brutus**   Stand ho!

**Lucilius**   Give the word, ho! and stand.

**Brutus**   What now, Lucilius, is Cassius near?

**Lucilius**   He is at hand, and Pindarus is come
5    To do you salutation from his master.

**Brutus**   He greets me well. Your master, Pindarus,
     In his own change, or by ill officers,
     Hath given me some worthy cause to wish
     Things done undone: but if he be at hand,
     I shall be satisfied.

10 **Pindarus**               I do not doubt
     But that my noble master will appear
     Such as he is, full of regard and honour.

**Brutus**   He is not doubted. A word, Lucilius;
     How he receiv'd you, let me be resolv'd.

15 **Lucilius**   With courtesy and with respect enough,
     But not with such familiar instance,
     Nor with such free and friendly conference,
     As he hath us'd of old.

enemies. Some of these smilers have mischief in their hearts, I fear.

[*They leave*]

## Scene 2

*A military camp near Sardis, outside* **Brutus***'s tent. Drums herald the appearance of* **Brutus, Lucilius,** *and their soldiers.* **Titinius** *and* **Pindarus** *meet them.*

**Brutus**  Halt!

**Lucilius**  [*passing the message down the line of soldiers*] Give the password! Halt!

**Brutus**  Well, now, Lucilius, is Cassius near?

**Lucilius**  He is close by, and Pindarus is here to give you his master's welcome.

**Brutus**  He sends his greetings by a good man. Your master, Pindarus, either through a change of heart or because he has incompetent officers, has given me considerable cause to wish that several things had never happened. But if he's here in person, I'll be given a proper explanation.

**Pindarus**  I do not doubt that my noble master will emerge with characteristic worthiness and honor.

**Brutus**  Undoubtedly. A word with you, Lucilius. Tell me how he received you.

**Lucilius**  Courteously, and with enough respect, but not with the customary familiarity, or the free and friendly conversation that we are used to.

**Brutus**                          Thou hast describ'd
A hot friend cooling. Ever note, Lucilius,
20  When love begins to sicken and decay
It useth an enforced ceremony.
There are no tricks in plain and simple faith;
But hollow men, like horses hot at hand,
Make gallant show and promise of their mettle;
25  But when they should endure the bloody spur,
They fall their crests, and like deceitful jades
Sink in the trial. Comes his army on?

**Lucilius**    They mean this night in Sardis to be quarter'd;
The greater part, the horse in general,
Are come with Cassius.

[*Enter* **Cassius** *and his Powers*]

30  **Brutus**                          Hark! he is arriv'd.
March gently on to meet him.

**Cassius**    Stand ho!

**Brutus**    Stand ho! Speak the word along.

**1st Soldier**    Stand!

35  **2nd Soldier**    Stand!

**3rd Soldier**    Stand!

**Cassius**    Most noble brother, you have done me wrong.

**Brutus**    Judge me, you gods; wrong I mine enemies?
And if not so, how should I wrong a brother?

40  **Cassius**    Brutus, this sober form of yours hides wrongs;
And when you do them –

**Brutus**                          Cassius, be content.
Speak your griefs softly; I do know you well.

**Brutus**    You have described a once-keen friend who's cooling off. When love begins to wane and die, Lucilius, you'll always find it resorts to strained politeness. There's no hypocrisy in plain and simple relationships. Shallow men, like horses raring to go, will flaunt their courage and seem promising, but when they have to answer to the spur, they drop their heads, and like deceitful wretches, they fail when put to the test.

[*The sound of marching can be heard*]

Is his army approaching?

**Lucilius**    They intend to make camp tonight in Sardis. The main section, mostly cavalry, has come with Cassius.

**Brutus**    Listen! He has arrived! March slowly forward to meet him.

[**Cassius** *appears, leading his troops*]

**Cassius**    [*to his men*] Halt!

**Brutus**    [*to his*] Halt! Pass the word down.

**1st Soldier**    Halt!

**2nd Soldier**    Halt!

**3rd Soldier**    Halt!

**Cassius**    [*straight to the point, in anger*] Most noble comrade, you have wronged me!

**Brutus**    [*his patience sorely tried*] Let the gods be judge! Do I wrong my enemies? If not, how could I wrong a brother?

**Cassius**    [*voice raised*] Brutus, this grave manner of yours hides wrongs. And when you commit them –

**Brutus**    Cassius, keep calm. Express your grievance quietly. I

Before the eyes of both our armies here,
Which should perceive nothing but love from us,
45    Let us not wrangle. Bid them move away;
Then in my tent, Cassius, enlarge your griefs,
And I will give you audience.

**Cassius**                              Pindarus,
Bid our commanders lead their charges off
A little from this ground.

50 **Brutus**    Lucius, do you the like; and let no man
Come to our tent till we have done our conference.
Lucilius and Titinius guard our door.

[*Exeunt*]

# Scene 3

*The same*

**Cassius**    That you have wrong'd me doth appear in this:
You have condemn'd and noted Lucius Pella
For taking bribes here of the Sardians;
Wherein my letters, praying on his side,
5    Because I knew the man, was slighted off.

**Brutus**    You wrong'd yourself to write in such a case.

**Cassius**    In such a time as this it is not meet
That every nice offence should bear his comment.

**Brutus**    Let me tell you, Cassius, you yourself
10    Are much condemn'd to have an itching palm,
To sell and mart your offices for gold
To undeservers.

know you well enough. Don't let us argue in front of both our armies. They should see nothing but harmony between us. Tell the men to move away. Then in my tent, Cassius, you can detail your complaints and I'll listen to them.

**Cassius**   [*tersely*] Pindarus. Order our commanders to move their troops away from here.

**Brutus**   Lucius, you do the same. Nobody is to enter our tent until we've finished our conference. Lucilius and Titinius – guard the door. [*They go.* **Brutus** *and* **Cassius** *are left alone. They enter* **Brutus**'s *tent.*]

## Scene 3

*The camp near Sardis. Inside* **Brutus**'s *tent* **Brutus** *and* **Cassius** *are alone.*

**Cassius**   [*it all comes out*] This is how you have wronged me. You have condemned and publicly denounced Lucius Pella for taking bribes here from the Sardians. My letters, appealing on his behalf because I knew the man, you slightingly ignored.

**Brutus**   [*coldly*] You wronged yourself when you wrote supporting him.

**Cassius**   At such a time as this, it isn't politic that every small offense should come in for criticism.

**Brutus**   [*not mincing words*] Let me tell you, Cassius, that you yourself are often accused of having an itching palm, selling and trading your political appointments for payment to worthless men.

161

**Cassius**              I an itching palm!
You know that you are Brutus that speaks this,
Or, by the gods, this speech were else your last.

15 **Brutus**   The name of Cassius honours this corruption,
And chastisement doth therefore hide his head.

**Cassius**   Chastisement!

**Brutus**   Remember March, the ides of March remember.
Did not great Julius bleed for justice' sake?
20   What villain touch'd his body, that did stab,
And not for justice? What, shall one of us,
That struck the foremost man of all this world
But for supporting robbers, shall we now
Contaminate our fingers with base bribes,
25   And sell the mighty space of our large honours
For so much trash as may be grasped thus?
I had rather be a dog, and bay the moon,
Than such a Roman.

**Cassius**              Brutus, bait not me;
I'll not endure it. You forget yourself,
30   To hedge me in. I am a soldier, I,
Older in practice, abler than yourself
To make conditions.

**Brutus**              Go to! you are not, Cassius.

**Cassius**   I am.

**Brutus**   I say you are not.

35 **Cassius**   Urge me no more, I shall forget myself;
Have mind upon your health; tempt me no farther.

**Brutus**   Away, slight man!

**Cassius**   Is't possible?

**Cassius**    Me, an itching palm! You know that only you, Brutus, could speak like that. Otherwise that speech would be your last, by god!

**Brutus**    The name of Cassius endorses this corruption, giving immunity from punishment.

**Cassius**    [*spitting the word out*] Punishment!

**Brutus**    [*unaffected by the anger shown*] Remember March! Remember the ides of March! Didn't the great Julius Caesar shed his blood for justice's sake? Who was so villainous as to stab his body, and not for justice? What? Shall any one of us who killed the world's most famous man for aiding thieves – shall we contaminate our fingers with contemptible bribes and sell our most senior positions, for so much filthy lucre as I can hold in my hand like this? [*He stretches out his fingers to demonstrate*] I'd rather be a dog and howl at the moon, than a Roman such as that.

**Cassius**    Brutus, don't provoke me! I won't stand it. You forget yourself when you limit my autonomy. I am a soldier; I am more experienced  and more capable than you are at handling things.

**Brutus**    Get away. You aren't, Cassius!

**Cassius**    I am.

**Brutus**    I say you are not.

**Cassius**    Don't push me or I'll forget myself. Watch it! Don't press me any more!

**Brutus**    [*turning on his heels*] Run away, little man!

**Cassius**    [*at the peak of self-control*] I can't believe it!

**Brutus**                              Hear me, for I will speak.
Must I give way and room to your rash choler?
40    Shall I be frighted when a madman stares?

**Cassius**    O ye gods, ye gods! Must I endure all this?

**Brutus**    All this? ay, more: fret till your proud heart break;
Go show your slaves how choleric you are,
And make your bondmen tremble. Must I budge?
45    Must I observe you? Must I stand and crouch
Under your testy humour? By the gods,
You shall digest the venom of your spleen,
Though it do split you; for, from this day forth,
I'll use you for my mirth, yea, for my laughter,
When you are waspish.

50 **Cassius**                              Is it come to this?

**Brutus**    You say you are a better soldier:
Let it appear so; make your vaunting true,
And it shall please me well. For mine own part,
I shall be glad to learn of noble men.

55 **Cassius**    You wrong me every way; you wrong me, Brutus.
I said, an elder soldier, not a better:
Did I say better?

**Brutus**                              If you did, I care not.

**Cassius**    When Caesar liv'd, he durst not thus have mov'd me.

**Brutus**    Peace, peace! you durst not so have tempted him.

60 **Cassius**    I durst not?

**Brutus**    No.

**Cassius**    What? durst not tempt him?

**Brutus**                              For your life you durst not.

**Brutus**    [*facing* **Cassius**; *in measured tones*] Listen, I'll be blunt. Must I give way to your quick temper? Take fright when a madman glares at me?

**Cassius**    [*white with tension*] Oh, gods, gods! Must I put up with all this?

**Brutus**    [*relentless*] All this? Yes, and more. You can fret till your proud heart breaks. Go and show your slaves how vile-tempered you are, and make your captives tremble. Must I flinch? Must I humor you? Must I stand here and cringe because you are irritable? By heavens, you can swallow your bad temper, however nasty that tastes. From now on, when you're testy, I'll amuse myself ridiculing you, laughing at you even!

**Cassius**    [*almost frothing at the mouth*] That really is too much!

**Brutus**    [*pressing on regardless*] You say you are a better soldier. Show it. Make good your boasts, and I'll be very pleased. Personally, I'm always glad to learn from noble men.

**Cassius**    You put me in the wrong in every way, Brutus. I said "a more experienced soldier," not a better one. Did I say "better"?

**Brutus**    Even if you did, I don't care.

**Cassius**    When Caesar was alive, he wouldn't have dared to cross me like this.

**Brutus**    Rubbish! You wouldn't have dared to provoke him so!

**Cassius**    [*unbelieving*] I wouldn't dare?

**Brutus**    No.

**Cassius**    [*bursting*] What – wouldn't dare provoke him?

**Brutus**    [*scornful*] Not on your life you wouldn't!

**Cassius**    Do not presume too much upon my love.
  I may do that I shall be sorry for.

65 **Brutus**    You have done that you should be sorry for.
  There is no terror, Cassius, in your threats;
  For I am arm'd so strong in honesty
  That they pass by me as the idle wind,
  Which I respect not. I did send to you
70  For certain sums of gold, which you denied me;
  For I can raise no money by vile means:
  By heaven, I had rather coin my heart,
  And drop my blood for drachmas, than to wring
  From the hard hands of peasants their vile trash
75  By any indirection. I did send
  To you for gold to pay my legions,
  Which you denied me: was that done like Cassius?
  Should I have answer'd Caius Cassius so?
  When Marcus Brutus grows so covetous,
80  To lock such rascal counters from his friends,
  Be ready, gods, with all your thunderbolts,
  Dash him to pieces!

**Cassius**      I denied you not.

**Brutus** You did.

**Cassius**     I did not. He was but a fool
  That brought my answer back. Brutus hath riv'd my heart.
85  A friend should bear his friend's infirmities;
  But Brutus makes mine greater than they are.

**Brutus** I do not, till you practise them on me.

**Cassius** You love me not.

**Brutus**      I do not like your faults.

**Cassius** A friendly eye could never see such faults.

**Cassius**  [*quivering*] Don't presume too much on my affection. I might do something I'd regret.

**Brutus**  You've already done something you'll regret! Your threats don't frighten me, Cassius. My integrity is such that they pass me by like the idle wind, which I disregard. I asked you for gold, which you denied me! I can't raise money by dishonest means. Heavens! I'd rather turn my heart to coinage and make drachmas from my blood, than steal small change from the calloused hands of peasants. I sent to you for gold to pay my legions, and you turned me down. Was that the real Cassius? Would I have answered Caius Cassius like that? When Marcus Brutus turns so miserly as to deny his friends some trashy coins, may the gods and all their thunderbolts be ready to dash him to pieces!

**Cassius**  I didn't turn you down.

**Brutus**  You did!

**Cassius**  I didn't. He was a fool who came back with that answer. Brutus has broken my heart. A friend should tolerate his friend's shortcomings. Brutus makes mine greater than they are.

**Brutus**  I didn't, till you tried them out on me.

**Cassius**  You are no friend.

**Brutus**  I don't like your faults.

**Cassius**  A friendly eye would never see such faults.

167

90 **Brutus**    A flatterer's would not, though they do appear
As huge as high Olympus.

**Cassius**    Come, Antony, and young Octavius, come,
Revenge yourselves alone on Cassius,
For Cassius is aweary of the world:
95 Hated by one he loves; brav'd by his brother;
Check'd like a bondman; all his faults observ'd,
Set in a note-book, learn'd, and conn'd by rote,
To cast into my teeth. O, I could weep
My spirit from mine eyes! There is my dagger,
100 And here my naked breast; within, a heart
Dearer than Pluto's mine, richer than gold:
If that thou be'st a Roman, take it forth.
I, that denied thee gold, will give my heart:
Strike, as thou didst at Caesar; for I know,
105 When thou didst hate him worst, thou lov'dst him better
Than ever thou lov'dst Cassius.

**Brutus**                                   Sheathe your dagger.
Be angry when you will, it shall have scope;
Do what you will, dishonour shall be humour.
O Cassius, you are yoked with a lamb
110 That carries anger as the flint bears fire,
Who, much enforced, shows a hasty spark,
And straight is cold again.

**Cassius**                          Hath Cassius liv'd
To be but mirth and laughter to his Brutus,
When grief and blood ill-temper'd vexeth him?

115 **Brutus**    When I spoke that, I was ill-temper'd too.

**Cassius**    Do you confess so much? Give me your hand.

**Brutus**    And my heart too.

**Cassius**                          O Brutus!

**Brutus**   A flatterer's wouldn't, even if they appear as high as Mount Olympus.

**Cassius**   Come, Antony, and young Octavius – come! Take your revenge on Cassius alone. Cassius is tired of this world. Hated by one he loves; taunted by his comrade; rebuked like a slave; all his faults analyzed, set down in a notebook, learned, and committed to memory to be thrown in my teeth. Oh, I could cry away my manliness! [*He takes his dagger from its sheath and offers it to* **Brutus**] There's my dagger. Here's my naked breast. Within it, there's a heart more precious than Pluto's mine, richer than gold. If you are a true Roman, cut it from me. I, who you say denied you gold, will give you my heart. Strike as you did at Caesar. I know that when you hated him most, you loved him better than you ever loved Cassius.

**Brutus**   [*relenting*] Put your dagger away. Be angry whenever you want, without restriction. Do whatever you like: I'll assume your insults are the outcome of temper. Cassius, you are allied to a tolerant sort of man, to whom anger is like flint's relationship to fire. Strike it some hard blows, it will produce a quick spark; but immediately afterward, it's cold again.

**Cassius**   Has Cassius lived his life only to be a mockery to Brutus whenever grief and his hot temper get the better of him?

**Brutus**   When I said that, I was ill-tempered too.

**Cassius**   [*brightening up*] Do you admit that? Give me your hand!

**Brutus**   And my heart too! [*They embrace in friendship*]

**Cassius**   [*overcome*] Oh, Brutus! [*He tries to speak but chokes*]

169

**Brutus**                                              What's the matter?

**Cassius**    Have not you love enough to bear with me,
When that rash humour which my mother gave me
Makes me forgetful?

120 **Brutus**                              Yes, Cassius; and from henceforth
When you are over-earnest with your Brutus,
He'll think your mother chides, and leave you so.

[*Enter a* **Poet** *followed by* **Lucilius, Titinius** *and* **Lucius**]

**Poet**    Let me go in to see the generals.
There is some grudge between 'em; 'tis not meet
125    They be alone.

**Lucilius**    You shall not come to them.

**Poet**    Nothing but death shall stay me.

**Cassius**    How now? What's the matter?

**Poet**    For shame, you generals! What do you mean?
130    Love, and be friends, as two such men should be;
For I have seen more years, I'm sure, than ye.

**Cassius**    Ha, ha! how vilely doth this cynic rhyme!

**Brutus**    Get you hence, sirrah! Saucy fellow, hence!

**Cassius**    Bear with him, Brutus; 'tis his fashion.

135 **Brutus**    I'll know his humour, when he knows his time.
What should the wars do with these jigging fools?
Companion, hence!

**Cassius**                          Away, away, be gone!

[*Exit* **Poet**]

**Brutus**    [*kindly*] What is it?

**Cassius**    Don't you love me enough to tolerate me, when that volatile nature I inherited from my mother makes me lose control?

**Brutus**    Yes, Cassius. And from now on, when you are remonstrating with me, I'll take it that it's your mother who is scolding, and leave it at that.

[*A* **Poet** *enters, followed by* **Lucilius**, **Titinius** *and* **Lucius**]

**Poet**    Let me enter the tent to see the generals. There is some difference of opinion between them. They should not be left alone.

**Lucilius**    You can't go in.

**Poet**    Nothing short of death will stop me.

**Cassius**    Well, now, what's the matter?

**Poet**    Shame on you, generals! What are you up to? Love, and be friends, as two such men should be; because I am some years older, surely, than either of you two.

**Cassius**    [*laughing – the tension relieved*] Ha! Ha! What a rotten poet this fellow is!

**Brutus**    [*joining in the fun*] Off you go, fellow! Cheeky fellow – depart!

**Cassius**    [*making a point*] Bear with him, Brutus. It's his disposition!

**Brutus**    I'll recognize his oddities when he masters his craft! What place in war is there for stupid rhymesters? Off you go, friend!

**Cassius**    [*ushering him out*] Away with you! Hence! [*The two men share the joke, then sober up and get down to business*]

**Brutus**    Lucilius and Titinius, bid the commanders
Prepare to lodge their companies tonight.

140 **Cassius**    And come yourselves, and bring Messala with you
Immediately to us.

[*Exeunt* **Lucilius** *and* **Titinius**]

**Brutus**                    Lucius, a bowl of wine!

[*Exit* **Lucius**]

**Cassius**    I did not think you could have been so angry.

**Brutus**    O Cassius, I am sick of many griefs.

**Cassius**    Of your philosophy you make no use,
145    If you give place to accidental evils.

**Brutus**    No man bears sorrow better. Portia is dead.

**Cassius**    Ha? Portia?

**Brutus**    She is dead.

**Cassius**    How 'scap'd I killing, when I cross'd you so?
150    O insupportable and touching loss!
Upon what sickness?

**Brutus**                    Impatient of my absence,
And grief that young Octavius with Mark Antony
Have made themselves so strong; for with her death
That tidings came. With this she fell distract,
155    And, her attendants absent, swallow'd fire.

**Cassius**    And died so?

**Brutus**                    Even so.

**Cassius**                                O ye immortal gods!

**Brutus**   Lucilius and Titinius, order the commanders to set up camp tonight.

**Cassius**   And come yourselves, and bring Messala with you immediately to us.

[**Lucilius** *and* **Titinius** *leave*]

**Brutus**   Lucius, bring a bowl of wine.

[**Lucius** *leaves*]

**Cassius**   I didn't know you could be so angry.

**Brutus**   [*for the first time giving in to his feelings*] Oh, Cassius! I'm sick with grief.

**Cassius**   You aren't making use of your stoic philosophy if you let bad luck get you down.

**Brutus**   Nobody bears sorrow better. [*He pauses*] Portia is dead.

**Cassius**   What, Portia?

**Brutus**   She is dead.

**Cassius**   [*dismayed*] How did I escape with my life when I vexed you so? Oh, what a devastating and grievous loss! What did she die of?

**Brutus**   Worry over my absence, and distress on hearing that young Octavius and Mark Antony have allied: news of that came just before her death. It made her lose her reason. When she was left unattended, she put hot coal in her mouth and choked.

**Cassius**   And died?

**Brutus**   She did.

**Cassius**   [*appalled*] Oh, immortal gods!

173

[*Enter* **Lucius** *with wine and taper*]

**Brutus**    Speak no more of her. Give me a bowl of wine.
In this I bury all unkindness, Cassius.

**Cassius**    My heart is thirsty for that noble pledge.
160    Fill, Lucius, till the wine o'erswell the cup.
I cannot drink too much of Brutus' love.

[*Exit* **Lucius**]

[*Enter* **Titinius** *and* **Messala**]

**Brutus**    Come in, Titinius. Welcome, good Messala.
Now sit we close about this taper here,
And call in question our necessities.

**Cassius**    Portia, art thou gone?

165 **Brutus**                                    No more, I pray you.
Messala, I have here received letters,
That young Octavius and Mark Antony
Come down upon us with a mighty power,
Bending their expedition toward Philippi.

170 **Messala**    Myself have letters of the self-same tenor.

**Brutus**    With what addition?

**Messala**    That by proscription and bills of outlawry
Octavius, Antony, and Lepidus
Have put to death an hundred senators.

175 **Brutus**    Therein our letters do not well agree.
Mine speak of seventy senators that died
By their proscriptions, Cicero being one.

**Cassius**    Cicero one?

[**Lucius** *returns with wine and candles*]

**Brutus**   Don't let's talk about her any more. Give me a bowl of wine. I'll drown all my resentment, Cassius. [*He drinks deeply*]

**Cassius**   My heart reciprocates. Lucius, fill the cup till the wine overflows. [*He too takes a long draught*] I cannot drink too much of Brutus's love.

[**Lucius** *leaves.* **Titinius** *and* **Messala** *enter*]

**Brutus**   Come in, Titinius. Welcome, good Messala. Let's sit together around this candle and get our strategy planned.

**Cassius**   [*still haunted by* **Portia**'s *death*] Portia, are you dead?

**Brutus**   [*the general now*] Please, no more. [*To his officers*] Messala, I've had letters saying that young Octavius and Mark Antony are converging on us with a mighty army, moving their forces toward Philippi.

**Messala**   I've had letters to the same effect.

**Brutus**   Anything further?

**Messala**   That Octavius, Antony and Lepidus have issued official warrants and put to death a hundred senators.

**Brutus**   In that respect our letters differ. Mine speak of seventy senators who died by their warrants, Cicero being one.

**Cassius**   [*dismayed*] Cicero one?

## Act four    Scene 3

The following passage may be printed in some editions of the play. It appears to be a first draft which Shakespeare intended to delete. The news of Portia's death has already been announced and discussed earlier. Some experts think both passages should stand.

**Messala**                    Cicero is dead,
And by that order of proscription.
180  (Had you your letters from your wife, my lord?

**Brutus**  No, Messala.

**Messala**  Nor nothing in your letter writ of her?

**Brutus**  Nothing, Messala.

**Messala**                    That, methinks, is strange.

**Brutus**  Why ask you? Hear you aught of her in yours?

185 **Messala**  No, my lord.

**Brutus**  Now as you are a Roman, tell me true.

**Messala**  Then like a Roman bear the truth I tell;
For certain she is dead, and by strange manner.

**Brutus**  Why, farewell, Portia. We must die, Messala.
190  With meditating that she must die once,
I have the patience to endure it now.

**Messala**  Even so great men great losses should endure.

**Cassius**  I have as much of this in art as you,
But yet my nature could not bear it so.


195 **Brutus**  Well, to our work alive. What do you think
Of marching to Philippi presently?

**Cassius**  I do not think it good.

**Brutus**                    Your reason?

**Cassius**                              This it is:
'Tis better that the enemy seek us;

**Messala**   Cicero is dead, by order of that warrant. [*To* **Brutus**] Have you had letters from your wife, my lord?

**Brutus**   No, Messala.

**Messala**   And there's nothing in your letters mentioning her?

**Brutus**   Nothing, Messala.

**Messala**   That's strange, isn't it?

**Brutus**   Why do you ask? Is there anything about her in yours?

**Messala**   No, my lord.

**Brutus**   As a Roman – tell me the truth.

**Messala**   Take the truth, then, like a Roman. She is dead, beyond all doubt. She died [ *he lowers his voice*] unusually.

**Brutus**   Why, farewell, Portia. We all must die, Messala. Knowing that she must die sometime, I have the courage to endure it now.

**Messala**   That's just how great men should endure great losses –

**Cassius**   Theoretically, I have as much stoicism as you, but I couldn't bear news like that.

**Brutus**   Well, to return to the work of the living. What do you think of marching to Philippi immediately?

**Cassius**   It's not a good idea.

**Brutus**   What's your reason?

**Cassius**   It's this. It's better that the enemy looks for us. That

So shall he waste his means, weary his soldiers,
200 Doing himself offence, whilst we, lying still,
Are full of rest, defence, and nimbleness.

**Brutus**    Good reasons must of force give place to better.
The people 'twixt Philippi and this ground
Do stand but in a forc'd affection;
205 For they have grudg'd us contribution.
The enemy, marching along by them,
By them shall make a fuller number up,
Come on refresh'd, new-added, and encourag'd;
From which advantage shall we cut him off
210 If at Philippi we do face him there,
These people at our back.

**Cassius**                                   Hear me, good brother.

**Brutus**    Under your pardon. You must note beside
That we have tried the utmost of our friends,
Our legions are brim-full, our cause is ripe:
215 The enemy increaseth every day;
We, at the height, are ready to decline.
There is a tide in the affairs of men,
Which, taken at the flood, leads on to fortune;
Omitted, all the voyage of their life
220 Is bound in shallows and in miseries.
On such a full sea are we now afloat,
And we must take the current when it serves,
Or lose our ventures.

**Cassius**                       Then, with your will, go on;
We'll along ourselves, and meet them at Philippi.

225 **Brutus**    The deep of night is crept upon our talk,
And nature must obey necessity,
Which we will niggard with a little rest.
There is no more to say?

way, he'll use up his resources, tire his soldiers, harming himself while we, staying put, will be rested, on the defensive and fresh.

**Brutus**    Good reasons must of necessity take second place to better ones. The people between Philippi and here are friendly only because they're obliged to be; they've begrudged us aid. The enemy, marching through them, will pick up recruits, arrive refreshed and reinforced, and with spirits high. We'll prevent all this if we face him at Philippi, with these people behind us.

**Cassius**    May I say, good brother –

**Brutus**    [*cutting him short*] Forgive me. [*Proceeding*] You must also take into account the fact that we have had all we can expect from our friends; our forces are at their maximum; our cause is at its peak. The enemy gets stronger every day. We are at our best, and ready to decline. Once in a lifetime, an opportunity occurs which, grasped, leads on to fortune. Missed, the rest of one's life is dull or even wretched. That's how things are today – riding in our favor – and either we seize our opportunity when it's here, or lose everything.

**Cassius**    [*conceding*] Since that's what you want, go forward. We'll do the same and meet them at Philippi.

**Brutus**    It's getting very late, and of necessity we must concede to nature a few short hours of sleep. Anything else?

**Cassius**                          No more. Good night.
  Early tomorrow will we rise, and hence.

**Brutus**    Lucius!

  [*Enter* **Lucius**]

                    My gown.

                                    [*Exit* **Lucius**]

230                                 Farewell, good Messala.
  Goodnight, Titinius. Noble, noble Cassius,
  Goodnight, and good repose.

**Cassius**                          O my dear brother,
  This was an ill beginning of the night.
  Never come such division 'tween our souls!
  Let it not, **Brutus**.

  [*Enter* **Lucius** *with the gown*]

235 **Brutus**                  Everything is well.

**Cassius**    Goodnight, my lord.

**Brutus**                          Goodnight, good brother.

**Titinius** ⎤
**Messala**  ⎦ Goodnight, Lord Brutus.

**Brutus**                              Farewell, every one.

                              [*Exeunt all but* **Brutus**]

  Give me the gown. Where is thy instrument?

**Lucius**    Here in the tent.

**Cassius**   Nothing. Good night. We'll rise early tomorrow morning and set off.

**Brutus**   Lucius!

[**Lucius** *enters*]

Give me my gown.

[**Lucius** *leaves*]

Farewell, good Messala. Goodnight, Titinius. Noble, noble Cassius, good night and sleep well.

**Cassius**   Dear brother, that was a nasty start to the evening. May we never again be divided like that! Don't allow it, Brutus.

[**Lucius** *returns with the gown*]

**Brutus**   Everything is fine.

**Cassius**   Goodnight, my lord.

**Brutus**   Goodnight, good brother.

**Titinius**
**Messala** } Goodnight, Lord Brutus.

**Brutus**   Farewell, everyone.

[**Cassius, Titinius** *and* **Messala** *leave*]

[*To* **Lucius**] Give me the gown. Where is your lute?

**Lucius**   [*very tired*] Here in the tent.

**Brutus**                                        What, thou speak'st drowsily?
240    Poor knave, I blame thee not; thou art o'er-watch'd.
       Call Claudius and some other of my men;
       I'll have them sleep on cushions in my tent.

**Lucius**    Varro and Claudius!

[*Enter* **Varro** *and* **Claudius**]

**Varro**    Calls my lord?

245 **Brutus**    I pray you, sirs, lie in my tent and sleep.
       It may be I shall raise you by and by
       On business to my brother Cassius.

**Varro**    So please you, we will stand and watch your pleasure.

**Brutus**    I will not have it so; lie down, good sirs;
250    It may be I shall otherwise bethink me.

[**Varro** *and* **Claudius** *lie down*]

       Look, Lucius, here's the book I sought for so;
       I put it in the pocket of my gown.

**Lucius**    I was sure your lordship did not give it me.

**Brutus**    Bear with me, good boy, I am much forgetful.
255    **Canst thou hold up thy heavy eyes awhile,**
       And touch thy instrument a strain or two?

**Lucius**    Ay, my lord, an't please you.

**Brutus**                                        It does, my boy.
       **I trouble thee too much, but thou art willing.**

**Lucius**    It is my duty, sir.

260 **Brutus**    I should not urge thy duty past thy might;
       I know young bloods look for a time of rest.

**Brutus**  You sound sleepy. Poor lad, I can't blame you. You are
up too late. Call Claudius and another of my men. I'll get them
to sleep on cushions in my tent.

**Lucius**  [*calling*] Varro! Claudius!

[*Enter* **Varro** *and* **Claudius**]

**Varro**  You called, my lord?

**Brutus**  I'd be obliged, sirs, if you would lie in my tent to sleep. I
might wake you later to communicate with Cassius.

**Varro**  By all means – we'll keep awake and wait for your
instructions.

**Brutus**  [*kindly*] I can't have that. Lie down, gentlemen. I could
easily change my mind.

[**Varro** *and* **Claudius** *settle down to sleep*]

Look, Lucius! [*Showing him a book*] Here's the book I was
looking for! I must have put it in the pocket of my gown.

**Lucius**  I was sure your lordship hadn't given it to me.

**Brutus**  Bear with me, lad. I'm getting forgetful. Can you keep
your eyes open for a short while and play something?

**Lucius**  Yes, my lord, if you wish.

**Brutus**  I do, my boy. I'm troubling you too much, but you are
willing.

**Lucius**  It is my duty, sir.

**Brutus**  I shouldn't press duty on you, past your strength. I
know young people like some rest.

**Lucius**    I have slept, my lord, already.

**Brutus**    It was well done, and thou shalt sleep again;
I will not hold thee long. If I do live,
265    I will be good to thee.

[*Music and a song*]

This is a sleepy tune. O murd'rous slumber!
Layest thou thy leaden mace upon my boy,
That plays thee music? Gentle knave, good night;
I will not do thee so much wrong to wake thee.
270    If thou dost nod, thou break'st thy instrument;
I'll take it from thee; and, good boy, good night.
Let me see, let me see; is not the leaf turn'd down
Where I left reading? Here it is, I think.

[*Enter the* **Ghost of Caesar**]

How ill this taper burns! Ha! who comes here?
275    I think it is the weakness of mine eyes
That shapes this monstrous apparition.
It comes upon me. Art thou any thing?
Art thou some god, some angel, or some devil,
That mak'st my blood cold, and my hair to stare?
280    Speak to me what thou art.

**Ghost**    Thy evil spirit, Brutus.

**Brutus**                                    Why com'st thou?

**Ghost**    To tell thee thou shalt see me at Philippi.

**Brutus**    Well; then I shall see thee again?

**Ghost**    Ay, at Philippi.

285 **Brutus**    Why, I will see thee at Philippi then.

[*Exit* **Ghost**]

**Lucius**  I have slept already, my lord.

**Brutus**  A good idea – and you will be able to sleep some more. I won't keep you long. If I should survive, I'll be good to you.

[**Lucius** *plays and sings softly, but gradually falls asleep*]

That's a sleepy tune. Oh, sleep! Have you summoned my boy, who plays music for you? Goodnight, my lad. I wouldn't be so hard as to waken you. [*He gently removes the instrument from* **Lucius**'s *fingers as he sleeps*] Nodding off, you'll break the lute. I'll take it from you. Good boy, good night. [*He turns to his book*] Let me see. Let me see. Isn't the leaf turned down where I left off reading? Here it is, I think.

[*The* **Ghost** of **Caesar** *enters*]

How dimly this candle burns. What? Who's this? Weak eyesight must be causing me to see this dreadful vision. It walks toward me. What are you? Some god, some angel, or some devil, making my blood run cold and my hair to stand on end? Tell me what you are!

**Ghost**  I am your evil spirit, Brutus.

**Brutus**  Why have you come?

**Ghost**  To tell you you shall see me at Philippi.

**Brutus**  Well, then I shall see you again?

**Ghost**  Yes. At Philippi.

**Brutus**  Why, I will see you at Philippi then.

[*The* **Ghost** *leaves*]

Now I have taken heart thou vanishest.
Ill spirit, I would hold more talk with thee.
Boy! Lucius! Varro! Claudius! Sirs, awake!
Claudius!

290 **Lucius**    The strings, my lord, are false.

**Brutus**    He thinks he still is at his instrument.
Lucius, awake!

**Lucius**    My lord?

**Brutus**    Didst thou dream, Lucius, that thou so criedst out?

295 **Lucius**    My lord, I do not know that I did cry.

**Brutus**    Yes, that thou didst. Didst see anything?

**Lucius**    Nothing, my lord.

**Brutus**    Sleep again, Lucius. Sirrah Claudius!
Fellow thou, awake!

**Varro**                    My lord!

**Claudius**                        My lord!

300 **Brutus**    Why did you so cry out, sirs, in your sleep!

**Both**    Did we, my lord?

**Brutus**                    Ay. Saw you any thing?

**Varro**    No, my lord, I saw nothing.

**Claudius**                        Nor I, my lord.

**Brutus**    Go and commend me to my brother Cassius.
Bid him set on his powers betimes before,
And we will follow.

305 **Both**                    It shall be done, my lord.

[*Exeunt*]

Now that I have my courage back, you've vanished. Evil spirit, I wanted a longer talk with you. [*Calling*] Boy! Lucius! Varro! Claudius! Gentlemen! Wake up! Claudius!

**Lucius**    [*snapping awake, startled*] The strings are out of tune, sir.

**Brutus**    He thinks he's still playing. [*Shaking him*] Lucius! Wake up!

**Lucius**    My lord?

**Brutus**    Was it a dream, Lucius, that made you cry out like that?

**Lucius**    My lord, I don't think I did cry out.

**Brutus**    Yes, you did. Did you see anything?

**Lucius**    Nothing, my lord.

**Brutus**    Go back to sleep, Lucius. That Claudius fellow! You there! Wake up!

**Varro**    My lord?

**Claudius**    My lord!

**Brutus**    Why did you both cry out in your sleep?

**Both**    Did we, my lord?

**Brutus**    Yes. Did you see anything?

**Varro**    No, my lord. I saw nothing.

**Claudius**    Nor I, my lord.

**Brutus**    Go convey my respects to my brother Cassius. Tell him to get his army moving very early in the morning, and we will follow.

**Both**    We'll do that, my lord.

[*They leave*]

# Act five

## Scene 1

*The Plains of Philippi. Enter* **Octavius**, **Antony** *and their Army*.

**Octavius**   Now, Antony, our hopes are answered.
You said the enemy would not come down,
But keep the hills and upper regions.
It proves not so; their battles are at hand;
5   They mean to warn us at Philippi here,
Answering before we do demand of them.

**Antony**   Tut, I am in their bosoms, and I know
Wherefore they do it. They could be content
To visit other places, and come down
10   With fearful bravery, thinking by this face
To fasten in our thoughts that they have courage;
But 'tis not so.

[*Enter a* **Messenger**]

**Messenger**          Prepare you, generals.
The enemy comes on in gallant show;
Their bloody sign of battle is hung out,
15   And something to be done immediately.

**Antony**   Octavius, lead your battle softly on
Upon the left hand of the even field.

**Octavius**   Upon the right hand I. Keep thou the left.

**Antony**   Why do you cross me in this exigent?

20 **Octavius**   I do not cross you; but I will do so.

# Act five

## Scene 1

*The Plains of Philippi.* **Octavius** *and* **Antony** *with their army encamped.*

**Octavius**   Our prayers are answered, Antony. You said the enemy would stay in the hills and higher ground, and not come down. That is not the case. Their armies are nearby. They mean to confront us at Philippi here, accepting our challenge before we've issued it.

**Antony**   I can put myself in their place, so I know why they're doing this. They'd rather not be here. They'll come down to us, full of bravado, hoping that this pretense will make us think they have courage. But it is not so.

[*A* **Messenger** *enters*]

**Messenger**   Prepare yourselves, generals. The enemy is coming toward us in confident show. The red flag is flying, signifying battle. Immediate action is required.

**Antony**   Octavius, lead your army slowly on the left side of the level ground.

**Octavius**   I'm on the right side. You can have the left.

**Antony**   Why do you argue with me at this crisis point?

**Octavius**   I'm not arguing with you. I'll do as I said.

[*Drum. Enter* **Brutus, Cassius,** *and their Army;* **Lucilius, Titinius, Messala,** *and others*]

**Brutus**    They stand, and would have parley.

**Cassius**    Stand fast, Titinius; we must out and talk.

**Octavius**    Mark Antony, shall we give sign of battle?

**Antony**    No, Caesar, we will answer on their charge.
25    Make forth; the generals would have some words.

**Octavius**    Stir not until the signal.

**Brutus**    Words before blows: is it so, countrymen?

**Octavius**    Not that we love words better, as you do.

**Brutus**    Good words are better than bad strokes, Octavius.

30 **Antony**    In your bad strokes, Brutus, you give good words;
Witness the hole you made in Caesar's heart,
Crying, 'Long live! hail, Caesar!'

**Cassius**                                        Antony,
The postures of your blows are yet unknown;
But for your words, they rob the Hybla bees,
And leave them honeyless.

35 **Antony**                                Not stingless too.

**Brutus**    O yes, and soundless too;
For you have stol'n their buzzing, Antony,
And very wisely threat before you sting.

**Antony**    Villains! you did not so when your vile daggers
40    Hack'd one another in the sides of Caesar:
You show'd your teeth like apes, and fawn'd like hounds,
And bow'd like bondmen, kissing Caesar's feet;
Whilst damned Casca, like a cur, behind
Struck Caesar on the neck. O you flatterers!

[*A drum sounds.* **Brutus, Cassius** *and their army appear,*
*attended by* **Lucilius, Titinius** *and* **Messala**]

**Brutus**   They've halted, and invite a parley.

**Cassius**   Halt, Titinius. We must ride out and speak to them.

[*In the other camp*]

**Octavius**   Mark Antony, shall we signal our intention to give
battle?

**Antony**   No, Caesar. We'll respond when they attack. Go
forward. The generals want to exchange a few words.

**Octavius**   Don't move until the signal.

[*The generals of both armies are now within shouting*
*distance*]

**Brutus**   Words before blows, eh, countrymen?

**Octavius**   Not that we like words better, as you do.

**Brutus**   Good words are better than bad sword strokes,
Octavius.

**Antony**   Your bad strokes, Brutus, are delivered with good
words. Witness the hole you made in Caesar's heart while at
the same time crying, "Long live! Hail, Caesar!"

**Cassius**   Antony, we've yet to know the kind of blows you
strike. As for your sweet words, you must have robbed the
hives at Hybla, where they're plentiful, and left the bees there
honeyless!

**Antony**   But not stingless too!

**Brutus**   Oh yes, and soundless. You've stolen their buzzes,
Antony, so now you very wisely threaten before you sting!

**Antony**   Villains! You gave no warning, when your vile daggers
clashed together in Caesar's body. You grinned like apes, and
fawned like hounds, and bowed like slaves, kissing Caesar's

191

45 **Cassius**    Flatterers? Now, Brutus, thank yourself
This tongue had not offended so today,
If Cassius might have rul'd.

**Octavius**    Come, come, the cause. If arguing make us sweat,
The proof of it will turn to redder drops.
50 Look,
I draw a sword against conspirators.
When think you that the sword goes up again?
Never, till Caesar's three and thirty wounds
Be well aveng'd; or till another Caesar
55 Have added slaughter to the sword of traitors.

**Brutus**    Caesar, thou canst not die by traitors' hands,
Unless thou bring'st them with thee.

**Octavius**                                      So I hope.
I was not born to die on Brutus' sword.

**Brutus**    O, if thou wert the noblest of thy strain,
60 Young man, thou could'st not die more honourable.

**Cassius**    A peevish school-boy, worthless of such honour,
Join'd with a masker and a reveller.

**Antony**    Old Cassius still!

**Octavius**                          Come, Antony; away!
Defiance, traitors, hurl we in your teeth.
65 If you dare fight today, come to the field;
If not, when you have stomachs.

[*Exeunt* **Octavius, Antony,** *and their Army*]

**Cassius**    Why now, blow wind, swell billow, and swim bark!
The storm is up, and all is on the hazard.

**Brutus**    Ho, Lucilius, hark, a word with you.

70 **Lucilius**    My lord?

feet – while that damned Casca came up like a mongrel dog from behind and stabbed Caesar in the neck. Oh, you flatterers!

**Cassius**  Flatterers! Now, Brutus, you have yourself to blame. If Cassius had had his way, that tongue would not be abusing us today.

**Octavius**  Come, come. To the point. If arguing makes us sweat, it's blood we'll need to shed to settle matters. [*He draws his weapon*] I draw my sword against conspirators. When do you suppose I'll put it back? Never – till Caesar's thirty-three wounds are properly revenged, or traitors' swords add me, a second Caesar, to their score.

**Brutus**  Caesar, you can't die by traitors' hands – unless they're your own.

**Octavius**  That's what I hope. I wasn't born to die on Brutus's sword.

**Brutus**  If you were the pick of your noble breed, young man, you couldn't die more honorably.

**Cassius**  A silly schoolboy, unworthy of such honor, allied with a playboy and a party-goer!

**Antony**  Still the same old Cassius!

**Octavius**  Come on, Antony. Let's go. [*To* **Brutus** *and* **Cassius**] We throw defiance in your teeth. If you dare fight today, come to the battlefield. If not, come when you've worked up the courage.

[**Octavius** *and* **Antony** *leave with their troops*]

**Cassius**  Well, now. Rough weather's ahead! The storm has gathered, and everything's at stake.

**Brutus**  [*beckoning*] Lucilius! Listen. I'd like a word with you.

**Lucilius**  My lord? [*They talk privately*]

**Cassius**    Messala.

**Messala**    What says my general?

**Cassius**                            Messala,
This is my birth-day; as this very day
Was Cassius born. Give me thy hand, Messala;
75    Be thou my witness that against my will,
As Pompey was, am I compell'd to set
Upon one battle all our liberties.
You know that I held Epicurus strong,
And his opinion; now I change my mind,
80    And partly credit things that do presage.
Coming from Sardis, on our former ensign
Two mighty eagles fell, and there they perch'd,
Gorging and feeding from our soldiers' hands,
Who to Philippi here consorted us.
85    This morning are they fled away and gone,
And in their steads do ravens, crows, and kites
Fly o'er our heads, and downward look on us,
As we were sickly prey; their shadows seem
A canopy most fatal, under which
90    Our army lies, ready to give up the ghost.

**Messala**    Believe not so.

**Cassius**                            I but believe it partly,
For I am fresh of spirit, and resolv'd
To meet all perils very constantly.

**Brutus**    Even so, Lucilius.

**Cassius**                            Now, most noble Brutus,
95    The gods today stand friendly, that we may,
Lovers in peace, lead on our days to age!
But since the affairs of men rests still incertain,
Let's reason with the worst that may befall.
If we do lose this battle, then is this

**Cassius**    Messala!

**Messala**    What says my general?

**Cassius**    Messala, today is my birthday. On this very day was Cassius born. Give me your hand, Messala. [*They shake hands, Roman fashion*] Be my witness that against my will — like Pompey — I'm obliged to gamble the liberty of our country on one battle. You know I was once a follower of Epicurus, who didn't believe in omens. I've changed my mind now. I partly believe things can be signs and portents. As we marched from Sardis, two mighty eagles landed on our leading standard-bearers, and there they perched, eating their fill and feeding from our soldiers' hands, staying with us till we reached Philippi. This morning they have flown away, and in their place ravens, crows and kites fly above our heads, and look down upon us as if we were sick prey. Their shadows are like a funeral canopy, signs of death, and our army lies beneath it, ready to give up the ghost.

**Messala**    Don't you believe it!

**Cassius**    I only partly believe it. I'm in good spirits and determined to meet all dangers resolutely.

**Brutus**    [*finishing his private talk*] Yes, indeed, Lucilius.

**Cassius**    Now, most noble Brutus, today the gods are well disposed, so that from being dear friends in peace, we can go on that way to old age! But as men's fortunes are always uncertain, let's consider what to do if the worst happens. If we lose this battle, this will be the very last time we shall speak

195

100    The very last time we shall speak together:
       What are you then determined to do?

       **Brutus**    Even by the rule of that philosophy
       By which I did blame Cato for the death
       Which he did give himself, I know not how,
105    But I do find it cowardly and vile,
       For fear of what might fall, so to prevent
       The time of life, arming myself with patience
       To stay the providence of some high powers
       That govern us below.

       **Cassius**                    Then, if we lose this battle,
110    You are contented to be led in triumph
       Through the streets of Rome?

       **Brutus**    No, Cassius, no: think not, thou noble Roman,
       That ever Brutus will go bound to Rome;
       He bears too great a mind. But this same day
115    Must end that work the ides of March begun;
       And whether we shall meet again I know not.
       Therefore our everlasting farewell take.
       For ever, and for ever, farewell, Cassius.
       If we do meet again, why, we shall smile;
120    If not, why then this parting was well made.

       **Cassius**    For ever, and for ever, farewell, Brutus.
       If we do meet again, we'll smile indeed;
       If not, 'tis true this parting was well made.

       **Brutus**    Why then, lead on. O, that a man might know
125    The end of this day's business ere it come!
       But it sufficeth that the day will end,
       And then the end is known. Come, ho! away!

                                              [*Exeunt*]

together. What have you decided to do then?

**Brutus**    Because I follow a certain rule of philosophy (why, I don't know) that makes me blame Cato for committing suicide, I find it cowardly and vile to cut life short for fear of what might happen. I'll patiently accept whatever the gods have planned for me.

**Cassius**    So if we lose this battle, you are content to be led in triumph through the streets of Rome?

**Brutus**    No, Cassius, no. Don't think, noble Roman, that Brutus will ever go to Rome in chains. His mind is above that. But today must end what the ides of March began. I don't know whether we shall meet again. Therefore, let's take an everlasting farewell. If we meet again, why, we'll smile. If not, why then this parting was appropriate.

**Cassius**    Forever and forever, farewell, Brutus. [*They embrace*] If we do meet again, we'll smile indeed. If not, it's true this parting was appropriate.

**Brutus**    Well then, lead on. If only one could know what the day has in store before it happens! But it's enough that the day will end, and then the end is known. Come then! Away!

[*They leave*]

## Scene 2

*The same. The field of battle. Enter* **Brutus** *and* **Messala.**

**Brutus**   Ride, ride, Messala, ride, and give these bills
Unto the legions on the other side.
Let them set on at once, for I perceive
But cold demeanour in Octavius' wing,
5   And sudden push gives them the overthrow.
Ride, ride, Messala; let them all come down.

[*Exeunt*]

## Scene 3

*Another part of the field. Enter* **Cassius** *and* **Titinius.**

**Cassius**   O, look, Titinius, look, the villains fly.
Myself have to mine own turn'd enemy:
This ensign here of mine was turning back;
I slew the coward, and did take it from him.

5 **Titinius**   O Cassius, Brutus gave the word too early,
Who, having some advantage on Octavius,
Took it too eagerly; his soldiers fell to spoil,
Whilst we by Antony are all enclos'd.

[*Enter* **Pindarus**]

**Pindarus**   Fly further off, my lord fly further off!
10   Mark Antony is in your tents, my lord.
Fly, therefore, noble Cassius, fly far off!

## Scene 2

*Philippi. The battlefield. Enter* **Brutus** *and* **Messala**.

**Brutus**   Ride, ride, Messala! Give these orders to the legions on
the other wing. [*The noise of war increases*] They must go into
battle immediately. Octavius's flank seems to me to be lacking
courage. A sudden push and we'd overthrow them. Ride, ride,
Messala. Tell them all to attack.

[*They leave*]

## Scene 3

*Another part of the battlefield.* **Cassius** *and* **Titinius** *enter amid
the din of battle.*

**Cassius**   [*distressed*] Oh, look, Titinius! Look! The villains are
running away! [*His men are seen fleeing for safety*] I've had to
turn against my own men. [*Pointing to a corpse*] This
standard-bearer of mine was turning back. I killed the coward
and took the flag from him.

**Titinius**   Oh, Cassius! Brutus gave the word too early. Having a
slight advantage of Octavius, he overreacted. His soldiers
started looting, while we are completely surrounded by
Antony's troops.

[**Pindarus** *enters*]

**Pindarus**   Retreat, my lord, retreat! Mark Antony has reached
your tents, my lord! So retreat therefore, noble Cassius,
retreat further!

**Cassius**    This hill is far enough. Look, look, Titinius!
Are those my tents where I perceive the fire?

**Titinius**    They are, my lord.

**Cassius**                                Titinius, if thou lov'st me,
15    Mount thou my horse, and hide thy spurs in him,
Till he have brought thee up to yonder troops
And here again, that I may rest assur'd
Whether yond troops are friend or enemy.

**Titinius**    I will be here again, even with a thought.

[*Exit*]

20  **Cassius**    Go, Pindarus, get higher on that hill;
My sight was ever thick. Regard Titinius,
And tell me what thou not'st about the field.

[*Exit* **Pindarus**]

This day I breathed first. Time is come round,
And where I did begin, there shall I end.
25    My life is run his compass. Sirrah, what news?

**Pindarus**    [*at a distance*] O my lord!

**Cassius**    What news?

**Pindarus**    Titinius is enclosed round about
With horsemen, that make to him on the spur,
30    Yet he spurs on. Now they are almost on him.
Now, Titinius; now some light. O, he lights too!
He's ta'en!

[*Shout*]

And, hark! they shout for joy.

**Cassius**   This hill is far enough. Look, Titinius, look! Are those my tents I can see on fire?

**Titinius**   They are, my lord.

**Cassius**   Titinius, do me a favor. Mount my horse, and ride him fast, till you've reached those troops there and back again, so I can rest assured whether they're friend or enemy.

**Titinius**   I'll be there and back in no time. [*He dashes off*]

**Cassius**   Pindarus, climb higher up that hill. My sight was always poor. Look carefully, Titinius, and tell me how things stand on the battlefield.

   [**Pindarus** *leaves in haste*]

This is the day on which I first drew breath. Time has come full circle. Where I began, there shall I end. My life has run its full circuit. [*Calling to* **Pindarus**] Fellow – what news?

**Pindarus**   Oh, my lord!

**Cassius**   What news?

**Pindarus**   Titinius is encircled by cavalry, who spur toward him. Yet he spurs on. Now they've almost reached him. Now, Titinius! Some dismount. Oh, he dismounts too! [*He groans*] He's captured! [*A shout is heard*] Listen, they shout for joy.

**Cassius**    Come down; behold no more.
O, coward that I am, to live so long,
35    To see my best friend ta'en before my face!

[*Enter* **Pindarus**]

Come hither, sirrah.
In Parthia did I take thee prisoner;
And then I swore thee, saving of thy life,
That whatsoever I did bid thee do,
40    Thou shouldst attempt it. Come now, keep thine oath.
Now be a freeman; and with this good sword,
That ran through Caesar's bowels, search this bosom.
Stand not to answer. Here, take thou the hilts,
And when my face is cover'd, as 'tis now,
45    Guide thou the sword. – Caesar, thou art reveng'd,
Even with the sword that kill'd thee.

[*Dies*]

**Pindarus**    So, I am free; yet would not so have been,
Durst I have done my will. O Cassius!
Far from this country Pindarus shall run,
50    Where never Roman shall take note of him.

[*Exit*]

[*Enter* **Titinius** *and* **Messala**]

**Messala**    It is but change, Titinius; for Octavius
Is overthrown by noble Brutus' power,
As Cassius' legions are by Antony.

**Titinius**    These tidings will well comfort Cassius.

**Messala**    Where did you leave him?

**Cassius**    Come down. Don't look any more. What a coward I am, to live so long that I see my best friend captured before my eyes!

[**Pindarus** *comes back*]

Come here, fellow. I took you prisoner in Parthia. In sparing your life, I made you swear that whatever I told you to do, you'd do it. Now you must keep your promise. Make yourself a free man. With this trusty sword, that ran through Caesar's stomach, dispatch me through the heart. Don't argue. Here, hold the hilt. When I cover my face – thus – thrust the sword. [**Pindarus** *does as he is ordered*; **Cassius** *slumps to the floor*] Caesar, you are revenged, and by the very sword that killed you. [*He dies*].

**Pindarus**    So I am free. But I wouldn't be, if I'd dared to have my own way. Oh, Cassius! [*He is overcome for a moment*] I'll go away from this country, where no Roman will ever find me.

[*He runs off.* **Titinius** *and* **Messala** *enter*]

**Messala**    It's equal exchange, Titinius. Octavius has been defeated by Brutus, just as Cassius's forces have been by Antony.

**Titinius**    Cassius will be pleased.

**Messala**    Where did you leave him?

55 **Titinius**                                    All disconsolate,
    With Pindarus, his bondman, on this hill.

**Messala**   Is not that he that lies upon the ground?

**Titinius**   He lies not like the living. O my heart!

**Messala**   Is not that he?

**Titinius**                      No, this was he, Messala,
60  But Cassius is no more. O setting sun,
    As in thy red rays thou dost sink to night,
    So in his red blood Cassius' day is set.
    The sun of Rome is set. Our day is gone;
    Clouds, dews, and dangers come; our deeds are done.
65  Mistrust of my success hath done this deed.

**Messala**   Mistrust of good success hath done this deed.
    O hateful Error, Melancholy's child,
    Why dost thou show to the apt thoughts of men
    The things that are not? O Error, soon conceiv'd,
70  Thou never com'st unto a happy birth,
    But kill'st the mother that engender'd thee.

**Titinius**   What, Pindarus! Where art thou, Pindarus?

**Messala**   Seek him, Titinius, whilst I go to meet
    The noble Brutus, thrusting this report
75  Into his ears. I may say thrusting it;
    For piercing steel and darts envenomed
    Shall be as welcome to the ears of Brutus
    As tidings of this sight.

**Titinius**                      Hie you, Messala,
    And I will seek for Pindarus the while.

                                            [*Exit* **Messala**]

80  Why didst thou send me forth, brave Cassius?
    Did I not meet thy friends, and did not they

**Titinius**   Very dejected, with Pindarus his slave, on this hill.

**Messala**   [*seeing the body of* **Cassius**] Isn't that he, lying on the ground?

**Titinius**   He doesn't seem to be alive. [*He looks closer*] Oh, my heart!

**Messala**   Is it he?

**Titinius**   No, it *was* he, Messala, but now Cassius is no more. [*He looks at the sky*] Oh, setting sun! Just as you turn red at nightfall, so in his red blood Cassius reaches his day's end. Rome's sun is set. We have had the best of our time. Ahead lies wretchedness. Our role is ended. Disbelief in my success has caused this.

**Messala**   Disbelief in great success has caused it. Why do false conclusions, offspring of melancholy, always seem so acceptable and right when they are not? Error is so easily conceived, but never does it run its full term: it always kills its parent.

**Titinius**   [*shouting*] Pindarus! Where are you, Pindarus?

**Messala**   Look for him, Titinius, while I go to meet the noble Brutus and thrust these tidings into his ears. "Thrust" is the word, for sharp steel and poisoned darts would be as welcome to the ears of Brutus as news of what we see here.

**Titinius**   Go then, Messala, and meanwhile I'll look for Pindarus. [**Messala** *rushes off. To the dead body of* **Cassius**] Why did you dispatch me, noble Cassius? Didn't I meet your friends? And didn't they put this victorious laurel wreath on

Put on my brows this wreath of victory,
And bid me give it thee? Didst thou not hear their shouts?
Alas, thou hast misconstrued every thing.
85   But hold thee, take this garland on thy brow;
Thy Brutus bid me give it thee, and I
Will do his bidding. Brutus, come apace,
And see how I regarded Caius Cassius.
By your leave, gods. This is a Roman's part:
90   Come, Cassius' sword, and find Titinius' heart.

[*Dies*]

[*Enter* **Brutus, Messala, Young Cato, Strato, Volumnius**
*and* **Lucilius**]

**Brutus**   Where, where, Messala, doth his body lie?

**Messala**   Lo, yonder, and Titinius mourning it.

**Brutus**   Titinius' face is upward.

**Young Cato**                    He is slain.

**Brutus**   O Julius Caesar, thou art mighty yet!
95   Thy spirit walks abroad, and turns our swords
In our own proper entrails.

**Young Cato**                    Brave Titinius!
Look where he have not crown'd dead Cassius.

**Brutus**   Are yet two Romans living such as these?
The last of all the Romans, fare thee well!
100   It is impossible that ever Rome
Should breed thy fellow. Friends, I owe more tears
To this dead man than you shall see me pay.
I shall find time, Cassius, I shall find time.
Come therefore, and to Thasos send his body:
105   His funerals shall not be in our camp,

my head, and ask me to give it to you? Didn't you hear their
shouts? Alas, you misunderstood everything. But wait. [*He
removes the laurel wreath*] Put this garland on your head.
Your Brutus asked me to give it to you, and I will carry out his
orders. Brutus, come quickly! See how I honored Cassius!
[*He picks up* **Cassius's** *weapon*] With your permission, gods
– Roman honor requires it. [*He holds the sword at his chest*]
Come, Cassius's sword, and find Titinius's heart! [*He kills
himself with a quick thrust*]

[*The noise of battle increases. Enter* **Brutus, Messala, Young
Cato, Strato, Volumnius** *and* **Lucilius**, *all very distressed*]

**Brutus**    Where, where is his body, Messala?

**Messala**    [*pointing*] There, yonder, and Titinius is mourning it.

**Brutus**    Titinius is facing upward.

**Young Cato**    [*rushing to check*] He's dead!

**Brutus**    Oh, Julius Caesar! You are mighty still! Your spirit is on
earth, turning our swords into our own bowels!

**Young Cato**    Brave Titinius! Look he has crowned dead
Cassius!

**Brutus**    Are there still two Romans living, such as these? [*He
salutes*] The last of all the Romans, farewell! Rome could not
possibly produce your equal. Friends, I owe more tears to
this dead man than you will see me pay. I shall find time,
Cassius, I shall find time. Let us go therefore, and send his
body to Thasos. We will not hold the funeral in our camp, in

Lest it discomfort us. Lucilius, come;
And come, young Cato; let us to the field.
Labeo and Flavius, set our battles on.
'Tis three a clock; and, Romans, yet ere night
110   We shall try fortune in a second fight.

*[Exeunt]*

## Scene 4

*Another part of the field. Enter* **Brutus, Messala, Young Cato,**
**Lucilius** *and* **Flavius.**

**Brutus**   Yet, countrymen, O, yet hold up your heads!

*[Exit]*

**Young Cato**   What bastard doth not? Who will go with me?
I will proclaim my name about the field.
I am the son of Marcus Cato, ho!
5   A foe to tyrants, and my country's friend.
I am the son of Marcus Cato, ho!

*[Enter* **Soldiers,** *and fight. Young Cato falls]*

**Lucilius**   And I am Brutus, Marcus Brutus, I!
Brutus, my country's friend; know me for Brutus!
O young and noble Cato, art thou down?
10   Why, now thou diest as bravely as Titinius,
And mayst be honour'd, being Cato's son.

**1st Soldier**   Yield, or thou diest.

case it damages morale. Come, Lucilius. And come, young
Cato. Let's return to the battlefield. Labeo and Flavius, signal
the attack. It's three o'clock and, Romans, before nightfall we'll
try our luck in a second fight.

[*They all leave*]


## Scene 4

*Another part of the battlefield.* **Brutus, Messala, Young Cato,
Lucilius** *and* **Flavius** *are fighting valiantly.*


**Brutus**   Hold your heads up high, countrymen! Hold them
high!

**Young Cato**   Who is of such base blood that he doesn't? Who'll
go with me? I'll shout my name around the field. [*At the top of
his voice*] I'm Marcus Cato's son! Enemy of tyrants! My
country's friend! I'm Marcus Cato's son! [*He fights with some
of Antony's soldiers and is killed*]

**Lucilius**   [*moving around the battlefield*] And I'm Brutus! Marcus
Brutus! Brutus, my country's friend! I'm Brutus, can't you see?
[*He sees a body on the ground*] Oh, young and noble Cato.
Have you fallen? You've died as bravely as Titinius, and as you
are   Cato's son, honor is yours.

[*An enemy* **Soldier** *challenges him*]

**1st Soldier**   Surrender or die!

**Lucilius**                              Only I yield to die:
There is so much that thou wilt kill me straight:
Kill Brutus, and be honour'd in his death.

15 **1st Soldier**    We must not. A noble prisoner!

[*Enter* **Antony**]

**2nd Soldier**    Room, ho! Tell Antony, Brutus is ta'en.

**1st Soldier**    I'll tell the news. Here comes the general.
Brutus is ta'en, Brutus is ta'en, my lord.

**Antony**    Where is he?

20 **Lucilius**    Safe, Antony; Brutus is safe enough.
I dare assure thee that no enemy
Shall ever take alive the noble Brutus.
The gods defend him from so great a shame!
When you do find him, or alive or dead,
25    He will be found like Brutus, like himself.

**Antony**    This is not Brutus, friend; but, I assure you,
A prize no less in wroth. Keep this man safe;
Give him all kindness; I had rather have
Such men my friends than enemies. Go on,
30    And see where Brutus be alive or dead;
And bring us word unto Octavius' tent
How every thing is chanc'd.

[*Exeunt*]

**Lucilius**   I only surrender to die. [*He offers a purse to the* **Soldier**] That's for you if you'll kill me now. Kill Brutus, and win honor through his death.

**1st Soldier**   We can't. Not a noble prisoner.

[**Antony** *approaches*]

**2nd Soldier**   Move back there! Tell Antony we've taken Brutus.

**1st Soldier**   I'll tell him. Here comes the general. We've captured Brutus! Brutus is captured, my lord!

**Antony**   Where is he?

**Lucilius**   Safe, Antony. Brutus is safe enough. I can assure you that no enemy will ever take the noble Brutus alive. May the gods save him from so great a shame! When you do find him — alive or dead, he'll be found like Brutus. Like the real Brutus.

**Antony**   [*to* **Soldier**] This is not Brutus, friend, but I assure you, he is a prize as valuable. Keep this man safe. Treat him well. I'd rather have such men my friends than enemies. Go and find out whether Brutus is alive or dead. Bring word to Octavius's tent how things have gone.

[*They leave*]

## Scene 5

*Another part of field. Enter* **Brutus, Dardanius, Clitus, Strato** *and* **Volumnius.**

**Brutus**    Come, poor remains of friends, rest on this rock.

**Clitus**    Statilius show'd the torch-light; but, my lord,
He came not back; he is or ta'en or slain.

**Brutus**    Sit thee down, Clitus. Slaying is the word;
5    It is a deed in fashion. Hark thee, Clitus. [*Whispers*]

**Clitus**    What, I, my lord? No, not for all the world.

**Brutus**    Peace then. No words.

**Clitus**                                    I'll rather kill myself.

**Brutus**    Hark thee, Dardanius.    [*Whispers*]

**Dardanius**                                Shall I do such a deed?

**Clitus**    O Dardanius!

10 **Dardanius**    O Clitus!

**Clitus**    What ill request did Brutus make to thee?

**Dardanius**    To kill him, Clitus. Look, he meditates.

**Clitus**    Now is that noble vessel full of grief,
That it runs over even at his eyes.

15 **Brutus**    Come hither, good Volumnius: list a word.

**Volumnius**    What says my lord?

**Brutus**                                    Why, this, Volumnius:
The ghost of Caesar hath appear'd to me
Two several times by night: at Sardis once,

# Scene 5

*Another part of the battlefield.* **Brutus, Dardanius, Clitus, Strato**
*and* **Volumnius** *are resting, exhausted.*

**Brutus**   Come then, we few remaining friends. Let's rest on this
rock.

**Clitus**   Statilius, our scout, waved his "all's-well" signal light
from our camp, as arranged – but, my lord, he hasn't returned.
He's either been captured or been killed.

**Brutus**   Sit down, Clitus. Killing's the word. It's all the fashion.
[*He whispers to* **Clitus**] A word, Clitus. [*He says something
which shocks*]

**Clitus**   What, me, my lord? No – not for all the world!

**Brutus**   [*his finger to his lips*] Hush, then. Say nothing.

**Clitus**   I'd rather kill myself.

**Brutus**   [*trying again*] Dardanius, a word. [*He whispers again*]

**Dardanius**   [*aghast*] Shall I do that? [**Brutus** *moves away*]

**Clitus**   [*a partner in the secret*] Oh, Dardanius!

**Dardanius**   Oh, Clitus!

**Clitus**   What terrible request did Brutus put to you?

**Dardanius**   To kill him, Clitus. Look – he's deep in thought.

**Clitus**   His cup of grief is full to overflowing, as his eyes well
show.

**Brutus**   [*beckoning*] Come here, good Volumnius. Listen a
moment.

**Volumnius**   What says my lord?

**Brutus**   Why, this, Volumnius. Caesar's ghost has appeared to
me on two occasions, at night. First at Sardis, and last night –

213

And this last night, here in Philippi fields.
I know my hour is come.

20 **Volumnius**                    Not so, my lord.

**Brutus**    Nay, I am sure it is, Volumnius.
Thou seest the world, Volumnius, how it goes;
Our enemies have beat us to the pit.
It is more worthy to leap in ourselves
25    Than tarry till they push us. Good Volumnius,
Thou know'st that we two went to school together:
Even for that our love of old, I prithee
Hold thou my sword-hilts, whilst I run on it.

**Volumnius**    That's not an office for a friend, my lord.

30 **Clitus**    Fly, fly, my lord, there is no tarrying here.

**Brutus**    Farewell to you; and you; and you, Volumnius.
Strato, thou hast been all this while asleep;
Farewell to thee too, Strato. Countrymen,
My heart doth joy that yet in all my life
35    I found no man but he was true to me.
I shall have glory by this losing day
More than Octavius and Mark Antony
By this vile conquest shall attain unto.
So fare you well at once; for Brutus' tongue
40    Hath almost ended his life's history.
Night hangs upon mine eyes; my bones would rest,
That have but labour'd to attain this hour.

[*Alarum. Cry within 'Fly, fly, fly!'*]

**Clitus**    Fly, my lord, fly!

**Brutus**                    Hence! I will follow.

[*Exeunt* **Clitus**, **Dardanius** *and* **Volumnius**]

here on Philippi fields. I know my time has come.

**Volumnius**    Not so, my lord!

**Brutus**    No, I'm sure it has, Volumnius. You see how things are.
Our enemies have beaten us into the ground. It's more
honorable for us to jump into our graves ourselves than wait
until they push us. Good Volumnius, you know we two went to
school together. For old times sake, I beg you to hold the hilt of
my sword, while I run on it.

**Volumnius**    [*shrinking away*] That's no duty for a friend, my
lord.

[*The sounds of battle get louder*]

**Clitus**    Run, my lord, run! You can't stay here!

**Brutus**    [*shaking hands*] Farewell to you, and you, and you,
Volumnius. Strato – you've been asleep all this time: farewell
to you, too, Strato. Countrymen, my heart rejoices that in all
my lifetime, I never met a man who was untrue to me. On this
day of defeat, I shall have more glory than Octavius and Mark
Antony can claim by their vile victory. So farewell, all of
you. The tongue of Brutus has almost spoken its last. My eyes
are heavy as at nighttime. My bones that labored to bring me
to this final hour seek rest.

[*Battle noises are now intense*]

**Clitus**    Run, my lord, run!

**Brutus**    Go ahead. I'll follow.

[**Clitus, Dardanius** *and* **Volumnius** *run off*]

I prithee, Strato, stay thou by thy lord.
45   Thou art a fellow of a good respect;
Thy life hath had some smatch of honour in it.
Hold then my sword, and turn away thy face,
While I do run upon it. Wilt thou, Strato?

**Strato**   Give me your hand first. Fare you well, my lord.

50   **Brutus**   Farewell, good Strato. Caesar, now be still;
I kill'd not thee with half so good a will.

[*Dies*]

[*Alarum. Retreat. Enter* **Antony, Octavius, Messala,
Lucilius** *and the Army*]

**Octavius**   What man is that?

**Messala**   My master's man. Strato, where is thy master?

**Strato**   Free from the bondage you are in, Messala.
55   The conquerors can but make a fire of him;
For Brutus only overcame himself,
And no man else hath honour by his death.

**Lucilius**   So Brutus should be found. I thank thee, Brutus,
That thou hast prov'd Lucilius' saying true.

60   **Octavius**   All that serv'd Brutus, I will entertain them.
Fellow, wilt thou bestow thy time with me?

**Strato**   Ay, if Messala will prefer me to you.

**Octavius**   Do so, good Messala.

**Messala**   How died my master, Strato?

65   **Strato**   I held the sword, and he did run on it.

**Messala**   Octavius, then take him to follow thee,
That did the latest service to my master.

Please, Strato, stay by me. You are a fellow well respected. Your life has not been without honor. Turn your face away and hold my sword while I run on it. Will you, Strato?

**Strato**   Give me your hand first. [*They shake*] Farewell, my lord.

**Brutus**   Farewell, good Strato. [**Strato** *holds the sword firmly and turns his face aside*] Caesar, rest in peace. I didn't kill you half so willingly. [*He runs on the sword and dies*]

[*A retreat sounds.* **Antony, Octavius, Messala** *and* **Lucilius** *enter*]

**Octavius**   Who's that man?

**Messala**   My master's servant. Strato, where is your master?

**Strato**   Free from the shackles you are in, Messala. The conquerors can only make a bonfire of him. Brutus defeated himself, and no man can claim the victory.

**Lucilius**   That's just how Brutus should be found. I always said he would never be taken alive.

**Octavius**   All those who served Brutus I shall enroll into my service. Fellow, will you work with me?

**Strato**   Yes – if Messala will recommend me to you.

**Octavius**   Do so, Messala.

**Messala**   [*inquiring first*] How did my master die, Strato?

**Strato**   I held the sword, and he ran on it.

**Messala**   Octavius, then take him on your staff. He did my master a final service.

**Antony**    This was the noblest Roman of them all.
          All the conspirators save only he
70        Did that they did in envy of great Caesar;
          He only, in a general honest thought
          And common good to all, made one of them.
          His life was gentle, and the elements
          So mix'd in him, that Nature might stand up
75        And say to all the world, 'This was a man!'

**Octavius**    According to his virtue let us use him,
          With all respect and rites of burial.
          Within my tent his bones tonight shall lie,
          Most like a soldier, order'd honourably.
80        So call the field to rest, and let's away,
          To part the glories of this happy day.

[*Exeunt omnes*]

**Antony**    [*over the body of* **Brutus**] This was the noblest Roman
of them all. All the conspirators except him did what they
did out of envy of great Caesar. He joined them only out of
loyalty to the people and for the common good. His life was
noble. He was such a mixture of parts, that Nature might rise
to her feet and proclaim to all the world: "This was a man!"

**Octavius**    Let us deal with him as his qualities deserve, with all
due respect and rites of burial. His body shall lie tonight in my
tent, like a true soldier, with full honor. Order the fighting to
stop, and let's depart to share the glories of this happy day.

[*Everyone leaves*]

# Activities

## Characters

Search the text (in either the original or the modern version) to find answers to the following questions. They will help you to form personal opinions about the major characters in the play. *Record any relevant quotations in Shakespeare's own words.*

### Julius Caesar

1 The first references to Caesar in the play reveal him as a controversial figure.
   a What do the common people of Rome think of him?
   b Why do the Tribunes, Marullus and Flavius, take an opposite view?
   c How does their view coincide with the one expressed later by Brutus?

2 From the brief introduction to Caesar at the beginning of *Act I Scene 2*, find evidence of
   a his superstitiousness (compare it with what Cassius says on the subject in *Act II Scene 1, lines 193–201* and find another example of it in *Act II Scene 2, lines 1–6*)
   b his pompousness
   c his self-assured manner
   and comment on
   d the way other people treat him and
   e his air of authority.

3 The Caesar of the play is aged about fifty-six. What do we learn about him as a younger man from the speeches of Cassius in *Act I Scene 2, lines 99–130?*

**4** On his return from the Lupercalian games (*Act I Scene 2, lines 180–86*)

  a Caesar is angry. Explain why, and say what this reveals of his character.

  b Caesar confides in Antony, a much younger man. Read carefully what he says to him, and decide

    i whether Caesar is a good judge of character

    ii whether Caesar is capable of fear

    iii whether Caesar is status-conscious

    iv whether Caesar has physical weaknesses such as Cassius earlier scorned and Casca later mentions.

**5** From Casca's description in *Act I Scene 2, lines 231–70* of Caesar's refusal of the crown, discuss

  a Caesar's skill as a politician in his dealings with the common people

  b his ruthlessness

  c his ambition.

**6** Read the soliloquy at the beginning of *Act II Scene 1*: "It must be by his death . . ." What are Caesar's shortcomings, according to Brutus?

**7** In *Act II Scene 1, lines 203–211* Decius mocks Caesar's weakness for flattery and claims he can exploit it.

Find the passage and give an example of Decius's technique in action.

**8** Caesar's arrogance is well demonstrated in *Act II Scene 2*, when he tells Calpurnia he will go to the Forum. Read his speeches and extract the phrases which reveal this aspect of his character.

**9** Prior to the entrance of Decius Brutus in *Act II Scene 2, line 57*, which of Caesar's pronouncements reveal that beneath his brave words there is perhaps a cowardly streak?

**10** In *Act II Scene 2*, Caesar could be accused of vacillation. Look up the meaning of the word, and say what evidence there is of its aptness.

Activities

11   Caesar habitually refers to himself in the third person. How revealing is this of an aspect of his character? Collect as many examples of this mannerism as you can find.

12   After the entrance of Decius Brutus in *Act II Scene 2, line 57*, Caesar's first three speeches show
  a  that he is always conscious of his public image
  b  that he affects to be fearless and straightforward
  c  that behind his bragging exterior there is a less confident man who has to explain away his weaknesses.
  Find the phrases which best illustrate these character traits.

13   Caesar accepts Decius Brutus's explanation of his dream and tells Calpurnia that he is ashamed of yielding to her entreaties (*Act II Scene 2, line 90, lines 105–107*). Read his speeches immediately afterward, when greeting the conspirators: do you think
  a  his affable remarks are genuine  or
  b  a way of covering up his embarrassment?
  Which line in particular could be described as excessively polite?

14   In *Act III Scene 1, lines 1–2*, Caesar has a brief exchange of words with the fortune-teller. Examine each of his short remarks and say what each can reveal of his character.

15   On his arrival at the Senate, Caesar has thirty lines (*Act III Scene 1, lines 35–48; 58–73*) to speak before Casca strikes his first blow. Find examples in those lines of:
  a  his pomposity
  b  his vanity
  c  his arrogance
  d  his affectation
  e  his pride
  Do you think Shakespeare had a dramatic purpose in showing Caesar at his worst immediately before the assassination? Explain this purpose.

**16** Although Caesar is killed in *Act III Scene 1, line 77,* his spirit is present in the remaining two acts, and his character is further delineated in the speeches that are made about him.

   a Read the speeches in *Act III Scene 1* in which Antony praises him both publicly (*lines 148–64; 183–213*) and privately (*lines 254–75*). What qualities are revealed?

   b Read the speeches of Brutus to the mob in the Forum (*Act III Scene 2, lines 13–31; 33–43; 53–9*). List the good and bad points about Caesar which he makes.

   c Examine Antony's funeral oration (*Act III Scene 2, lines 71–350*), and extract from it evidence of Caesar's former greatness, and his generosity.

**17** In his argument with Cassius in *Act IV Scene 3,* Brutus refers to Caesar in terms of both praise and censure. Find the speech, and decide whether

   a the praise is consistent with earlier reference to Caesar's qualities and

   b whether the criticism is so major that Brutus should have mentioned it earlier.

**18** Do the dying words of Cassius (*Act V Scene 3, lines 33–46*) and Brutus (*Act V Scene 5, lines 50–51*) influence your evaluation of Caesar's character?

**19** Critics have disagreed about Shakespeare's intentions in creating the character of Caesar out of the material he found in Plutarch. One says that Caesar is "a monstrous tyrant": another believes that Shakespeare undoubtedly wished us to admire him. What do you think?

**20** Antony says, "The evil that men do lives after them;/ The good is oft interred with their bones" (*Act III Scene 2, lines 73–4*). Does your own view of Caesar's character bear this out or contradict it?

## Brutus

1 From *Act I Scene 2* and *Scene 3* we learn a great deal about the character of Brutus. How do we know from it that he is
   a a man with a thoughtful disposition
   b a man who is widely respected in society
   c an honorable man
   d a man with a social conscience
   e a freedom-loving man
   f a man capable of being manipulated?

2 Brutus's soliloquy at the beginning of *Act II Scene 1* ("It must be by his death") shows he is a man who
   a puts the common good before personal feelings
   b tries to base his actions on reason.
   Find the evidence for this from his own words.

3 After deciding to join with the conspirators, Brutus refuses to swear an oath. Read the speech in *Act II Scene 1, lines 114–40,* in which he gives his reasons, and decide what this tells us of
   a his moral principles
   b his judgment
   c his political realism
   d his idealism.
   In his dealings immediately afterward with the conspirators, what further evidence can you glean about these attributes of his character?

4 Another aspect of the character of Brutus is shown toward the end of *Act II Scene 1*, when Portia questions him about his recent behavior. How does this conversation (*lines 234–302*) reveal
   a his introspective nature
   b his tenderness
   c his love and respect for his wife?

5 How does the final episode in *Act II Scene 1, lines 309–28* – the discussion with Ligarius – show that Brutus is
   a a natural leader
   b a man respected in the Roman community?

**6** a What does the Popilius Lena incident (*Act III Scene 1, lines 13–14*) tell us about the ability of Brutus to cope with a crisis?

 b How does this same quality show itself in the period immediately after the assassination but before the entry of Trebonius?

**7** The speech "Grant that, and then is death a benefit" (*Act III Scene 1, lines 103–10*) has been ascribed by some editors to Casca.

 a Explain why and

 b make out a case for attributing the speech to Brutus, because it is consistent with an aspect of his character.

**8** Consider the words and actions of Brutus immediately after the entry of Antony's servant in *Act III Scene 1, lines 138–43*. Find evidence of Brutus's

 a honorable qualities

 b inability to judge character

 c lack of practical wisdom

 d tendency to make ill-advised decisions

 e inclination always to have his own way.

**9** In his address to the mob in the Forum (*Act III Scene 2, lines 12–44*), Brutus speaks in prose, not blank verse. His words have been described as "a lecture."

 a Show from the speech that Brutus knows he enjoys the respect of Roman citizens.

 b Show that he believes the crowd is capable of making rational and just decisions.

 c Show that his speech is based on an appeal to reason and logic.

 d Show that he is proud of his patriotism and his republicanism.

 e Show that he wishes to act magnanimously.

 Comment on the wisdom of his approach and assumptions. Do you think it is reasonable to describe him as politically naive?

**10** The quarrel scene (*Act IV Scene 2*) has been belittled by the critic Thomas Rymer in the seventeenth century; praised by John Dryden, his contemporary, for its "masculinity" in the eighteenth century; admired as an example of dramatic genius in the nineteenth century (by Samuel Taylor Coleridge); and dismissed as "irrelevant" by the twentieth-century critic Henry Bradley. Read it carefully, and then decide for yourself

a whether Brutus is (i) unrealistic in expecting his allies always to act honorably or (ii) admirable in his inflexible attitude to corruption

b whether Brutus is (i) arrogant and insensitive toward Cassius at the beginning of the quarrel or (ii) properly firm and uncompromising

c whether Brutus (i) taunts Cassius or (ii) refuses to be browbeaten by him

d whether Brutus is (i) insultingly cold or (ii) admirably forthright

e whether Brutus's (i) "sober form . . . hides wrongs" or (ii) whether he is "armed so strong in honesty" that he cannot compromise.

Form an opinion of your own about the character of Brutus as it is revealed in the quarrel with Cassius from its beginning to its height.

**11** At the summit of the quarrel, a speech by Cassius totally alters Brutus's attitude. Look this up, and decide what aspect of Brutus's character is shown by this sudden change in his mood.

**12** The reconciliation between Cassius and Brutus leads to the revelation of Portia's death.

a Comment on Brutus's stoicism.

b Read the note in the text (page 176) which draws attention to a possible printing error. Supposing Shakespeare intended both passages to stand, what does the second reference to Portia's death add to our understanding of Brutus's character?

**13** After the reconciliation, the generals discuss military strategy (*Act IV Scene 3, lines 162–78; 195–224*). How does Brutus's contribution illustrate
  a his opinionated manner
  b his unwavering faith in his own powers of reason
  c his fatal tendency to draw wrong conclusions?

**14** After the military conference Brutus has dealings with his servant Lucius, and the soldiers Varro and Claudius (*Act IV Scene 3, lines 230–73; 287–305*). What more do we learn of the character of Brutus from the way he handles them?

**15** In *Act V Scene 1, lines 94–127*, Brutus and Cassius discuss the possibility of defeat. From what Brutus says, what do we learn about
  a his philosophy
  b his pride?
  Is there an inconsistency in what he says?

**16** After the first battle, Titinius and Cassius kill themselves. After the second (*Act V Scene 5, line 20*), Brutus says, "I know my hour is come."
  a Comment on the responses of Clitus, Volumnius and Strato to Brutus's approaches, and say what they tell us of Brutus and the esteem in which he is held.
  b Brutus claims (*Act V Scene 5, lines 36–7*) "I shall have glory by this losing day / More than Octavius and Mark Antony." Is this (i) true and (ii) does the comment shed any light on an aspect of his character?

**17** Read the speeches of Antony and Octavius which conclude the play. Do they do justice to the character of Brutus as you understand it?

**18** Most critics have admired the qualities of Brutus and concluded that Shakespeare intended him to be a tragic hero. But at least one prominent editor has found many of his attributes deplorable. List the case for and against Brutus as "the noblest Roman of them all."

19 Collect as many statements about Brutus and his qualities as you can find in the text (e.g.,"good Brutus"; "noble Brutus"; "gentle Brutus"; "thy honorable mettle," etc.). In what way does such a collection make sense of Caesar's dying words?

20 Collect together the references to his character made by Brutus himself. Are they, in your opinion,
   a justified; or is he
   b "merely talking big," as one critic expresses it?

## Cassius

1 From the first words Cassius addresses to Brutus in *Act I Scene 2, line 25*, show how he is
   a adept at appealing to other people's emotions
   b clever in concealing his own motives behind the reported opinions of others
   c accurate in delineating his own characteristics.

2 From the story which Cassius tells Brutus about Caesar, (*Act I Scene 2, lines 96–130*) and his subsequent comments before the re-entry of Caesar, select the words and phrases which reveal to us
   a his personal pride
   b his manly courage
   c his jealousy and/or hatred
   d his contempt
   e his bitterness
   f his passionate convictions
   g his obsequiousness
   h his envy

3 Read Caesar's analysis of Cassius's character in *Act I Scene 2, lines 191–211*, and
   a list the points he makes
   b comment on each as an accurate observation.

**4** Cassius delivers a revealing soliloquy at the end of *Act I Scene 2, lines 299–312*. Extract from it

    a evidence of his ability to manipulate others

    b evidence of personal resentment

    c evidence of deliberate intent to corrupt

    d evidence of his hardheadedness

    e evidence of his unscrupulous scheming.

**5** In the storm scene (*Act I Scene 3*) Cassius wins over Casca to the conspiracy. His approach (*lines 57–130*) is different from the one he employed to "seduce" Brutus.

    a Show how it is more physical than intellectual, and explain why.

    b Show how Cassius is more forthright.

    c Show how he plays on Casca's fear of the supernatural.

    d Show how it exhibits manly passion.

    e Show how it contains some effective playacting.

    f Show how it demonstrates his qualities of leadership among lesser men.

**6** In *Act II Scene 1*, in which Cassius wins over Brutus to the conspiracy, show evidence of

    a his tact

    b his ability to strike the right note when making his approach

    c his willingness to take second place when it suits him.

**7** What do we learn of Cassius's character from the Popilius Lena incident, at the beginning of the assassination scene (*Act III Scene 1, lines 13–14*)?

**8** Immediately after the assassination and before the entry of Antony (*Act III Scene 1, lines 80–146*), show how

    a he frequently echoes Brutus

    b he uses Brutus as a "front man"

    c he shrewdly identifies where danger lies, but tactfully defers to Brutus rather than cross him at a crucial time.

**9** After Antony's arrival (*Act III Scene 1, line 147*), note how Cassius responds to the challenge, and say

a why his first words to Antony (*lines 177–8*) are more politically effective than those of Brutus

b why he interrupts Antony's speech at the point when the latter says "How like a deer, strucken by many princes / Dost thou lie here!" (*lines 209–10*)

c why he takes Brutus to one side, and whether what he says confirms your opinion of his character.

**10** The quarrel scene (*Act IV Scene 3*) shows Cassius in many moods.

a *choleric*: what are the reasons for his anger, and are they justified?

b *tormented*: how does Brutus provoke him, and what does Cassius's restraint reveal of his personality?

c *passionate*: does the passion throw a new light on his character?

d *affectionate*: how does this show, and is it surprising?

e *jocular*: which episode brings out a flash of humor, and what is its purpose?

f *sympathetically emotional*: would you have expected him to react to Portia's death in the way he does? How does it compare with Brutus's own response?

g *dependent*: what evidence is there to show that in his relationship with Brutus, there is another side to Cassius than the one presented in the scenes before the assassination?

**11** In the battle scenes in *Act V*, what evidence can you find

a of Cassius's courage in adversity

b his ability to inspire loyalty

c his change of philosophic outlook

d his weak eyesight?

**12** a How far would the words used by Antony (*Act V Scene 5, lines 73–5*) about Brutus–"the elements / So mixed in him, that Nature might stand up / And say to all the world, 'This was a man!' "–apply to Cassius, taking all things into consideration?

b How far would you agree that Cassius deserves the words of praise in Brutus's speech over his dead body (*Act V Scene 3, lines 98–106*)?

## Antony

1 Antony is a developing character. He first appears briefly in *Act I Scene 2*.

a How would you describe him from his first lines of dialog with Caesar (*lines 5–10*)?

b How does Brutus describe him (*line 28*)?

c From Antony's assurances to Caesar about Cassius (*lines 193–4*), does he seem to be the kind of man Cassius later calls "a shrewd contriver" (*Act II Scene 1, line 158*)?

2 Cassius and Brutus disagree about Antony in *Act II Scene 1* (*lines 155–89*).

a Why does Cassius fear him?

b What is Brutus's assessment of Antony's character and potential?

c Which side does Trebonius take (*lines 190–91*), and why?

d From Caesar's references to him in *Act II Scene 2, lines 55, 116–17*, which view would seem to be the right one?

e Is the fact that Antony suspects nothing on the day of the assassination consistent with the popular opinion of his character?

3 After the assassination, Antony sends a servant to Brutus (*Act III Scene 1*).

a Examine the message (*lines 123–37*) carefully. What does it tell us of the man who sent it?

b Brutus and Cassius both comment on Antony's character and his likely course of future action (*lines 138–46*). To what extent are the compliments on the one hand and the suspicions on the other both right?

4 From Antony's first meeting with the conspirators after the assassination (*Act III Scene 1 line 147*), to his exit bearing Caesar's corpse (*line 297*), new dimensions to his character are revealed.

  a *As a diplomat*: What words does he use to describe Caesar's killers when in their presence, and what manner does he adopt in negotiating with them?

  b *As a tactician*: How does he contrive to align himself with the conspirators and anticipate possible criticism of his conduct at one and the same time?

  c *As a man of genuine emotion*: Examine his expressions of devotion to his late leader. Which would you cite as evidence of his sincerity?

  d *As a man of guile*: Antony's objective is to speak at Caesar's funeral; which of Brutus's qualities does he appeal to in order to achieve his goal?

  e *As a passionate and revengeful man*: From the start of his soliloquy at the end of *Act III Scene 1 (line 254)* to his exit, Antony shows that he has chosen not to accept "a place in the commonwealth."

    i Which words show that he has been acting a part?

    ii Which words show his determination to wreak vengeance?

    iii Which words spell out his innermost feelings, recently suppressed?

    iv Which words show him to be a strategist?

5 Until Caesar's assassination, Antony is a man of few words. In the funeral oration in *Act III Scene 2, lines 71–250*, he shows he has mastered the art of swaying a mob.

  a In his opening remarks ("Friends, Romans, countrymen, lend me your ears") how does he use (i) humility; (ii) fact; (iii) rhetorical questions; (iv) references to honor and ambition; (v) emotion to win over the volatile crowd?

    b Antony's second step is to announce the existence of Caesar's will (*line 126*). What is so clever about his pretending not to want to read it?

    c What does he gain by switching attention to Caesar's corpse?

    d Examine the speech beginning "Good friends, sweet friends, let me not stir you up / To such a sudden flood of mutiny" (*lines 206–27*). Trace the words and phrases that you think Antony uses to trigger off desirable responses in the crowd.

    e What does Antony achieve by leaving the contents of the will to the last?

    f Which of his concluding words show that Antony is indeed the "shrewd contriver" Cassius always said he was?

**6** In *Act IV Scene 1*, Antony reveals that he is
    a ruthless and callous
    b unscrupulous and cynical
    c scornful and arrogant.
    Find evidence from his speeches in confirmation.

**7** In *Act V Scene 1, lines 1–20*, Octavius criticizes Antony for a false prediction and refuses to take orders from him, but they do not quarrel. Comment on this from the point of view of
    a Antony's generalship
    b Antony's self-control.

**8** In the exchange of words before the battle (*Act V Scene 1, lines 21–63*) would you
    a agree or disagree that Antony is more than a match for the taunts of Brutus and Cassius?
    b Do you think his retorts are evidence of his determination to wreak vengeance on behalf of Caesar?

**9** In his last two appearances in the play (*Act V Scene 4, lines 26–29, and Scene 5, lines 68–75*), Antony is depicted as magnanimous in victory. Do you regard this as

a a dramatic inconsistency or

b a rounding-off of the process of his development as a major figure?

10 In another of Shakespeare's plays ("*Macbeth*," *Act III Scene 1*) these words occur:

"under him
My genius is rebuked, as it is said
Mark Antony's was by Caesar."

(This is a way of saying that Mark Antony could not be a full person in his own right while Caesar was alive.)

Reviewing the play as a whole, would you say that the Antony of *Julius Caesar* is a confirmation of the legend Macbeth refers to?

## Casca

1 Casca speaks two lines only at the beginning of *Act I Scene 2*, before Caesar leaves for the Lupercalia.

a What opinion would you form from them of his relationship to Caesar, and his attitude to the society in which he lives?

b Comment on the fact that Casca is eventually to stab Caesar in the back.

2 Casca's report of Caesar's refusal of the crown *Act I Scene 2*, *lines 217–70*, is delivered in "his sour fashion."

a How can you tell that Cassius and Brutus humor him?

b What is sour about
   i his references to the mob
   ii his description of Caesar's refusals?

c How does Shakespeare convey the impression that Casca is cynical and offhand?

d Cassius makes a cryptic remark about the falling-sickness. Casca does not rise to the bait. Why?

   e Casca uses a number of colloquial expressions, such as "I can as well be hanged as tell the manner of it" (*line 231*). Find others and say how they vividly convey Casca's character.

   f Casca twice refers to things he might have done, but didn't. Find these, and say what you deduce about his courage.

   g What phrase of Casca's conveys the impression that he wants to be known as a nonintellectual?

   h Do you think it is significant that Casca reports the deaths of Marullus and Flavius, but makes no comment?

   i Casca twice uses the word "foolery." What does he hope will be the effect on his listeners?

   j What impression of Casca do you gain from the way in which he responds to the dinner invitation?

**3** Does the discussion between Brutus and Cassius about Casca's character (*Act I Scene 2, lines 287–96*)

   a accord with your own view of Casca's manner

   b make Casca more or less likable?

**4** a Does Casca's behavior in the storm (*Act I Scene 3*) merit Cassius's blunt words of criticism or

   b is it – like his " 'Tis Caesar that you mean, is it not, Cassius?" (*line 79*) – an example of the "tardy form" that he "puts on," as some critics have said?

   c Casca says he is "no fleering tell tale" (*line 117*). But some member of the conspiracy must have betrayed the secret of the assassination plot to Artemidorus, so that he could write the warning note of *Act II Scene 3*. From your understanding of Casca's character, could he have been the one?

   d Why is Casca's reason for wanting Brutus to join the faction consistent with his character as we know it?

**5** Look up the discussion in *Act II Scene 1, lines 141–53*, about the suitability of Cicero as a member of the group. Comment on Casca's contribution.

6 Both Cassius and Cinna turn to Casca in *Act III Scene 1, lines 19 and 30*, as the man of action. How is this consistent with what Cassius says about him in *Act I Scene 2, lines 291–95*?

7 Antony refers to "my valiant Casca" in *Act III Scene 1, line 188*; "the envious Casca" in *Act III Scene 2, line 173*; "damned Casca" in *Act V Scene 1, line 43*. Check the circumstances in which each remark is made, and say whether Casca's contribution to the plot against Caesar is of a different order from that of Brutus and Cassius.

## Decius Brutus

1 We meet Decius Brutus for the first time in *Act II Scene 1, line 101*; he boasts that he can "o'ersway" Caesar (*line 203*). What is his technique based on, and how does he execute it in practice?

2 Decius speaks five times in the assassination scene (*Act III Scene 1, lines 4–5, 27, 75, 84, 119*). On each occasion, what he says is of importance to the management of affairs. Explain the significance of each of his remarks.

## Portia and Calpurnia

1 Portia's caring concern for Brutus is clear from her speeches in *Act II Scene 1, lines 233–97*.
   a How many times did she press Brutus for an explanation of his withdrawn conduct?
   b What phrase of hers shows that she is understanding and tolerant when her husband is out of sorts?
   c Portia has a clear conception of what true marriage implies. Explain what it is, and comment on her relationship to her husband.
   d Portia is aware she is living in a man's world. What are her claims for an equal share of Brutus's secrets?

2　a　Calpurnia makes a brief public appearance in *Act I Scene 2*, but does not speak. Caesar does: what might an observer think about their relationship?

　　b　Calpurnia is next seen at home – *Act II Scene 2* – where she shows concern for Caesar's safety.

　　　i　Does Caesar's manner alter when in private conversation with his wife?

　　　ii　Before Decius Brutus enters, Calpurnia succeeds in changing Caesar's mind. What kinds of influence does she bring to bear?

　　　iii　In changing his mind, Caesar says, "Mark Antony shall say I am not well." When Calpurnia instructs Decius Brutus to "say he is sick," Caesar bridles. Do you think this could be significant in interpreting their relationship?

3　Compare Portia and Calpurnia

　a　as women

　b　as wives.

## The Commoners

1　a　Marullus and Flavius (*Act I Scene 1*) identify many of the characteristics of the common people. Which are acted out later in the play?

　　b　The commoners in this scene are good humored, possessed of a conscience, and (according to the Tribunes) misguided. Find examples of these three characteristics.

2　Casca (*Act I Scene 2*) describes the commoners in action at the Forum.

　a　Why did they anger Caesar?

　b　How did they show their feelings?

　c　What words does Casca use to describe them?

　d　Which three of their vulgar characteristics does Casca cite?

　e　What examples does he give of their gullibility?

3 In the funeral scene (*Act III Scene 2*), the commoners hear Brutus speak first. Which of their remarks show that they have failed to understand the reasons why Caesar was killed?

4 Antony shows a masterly control over the fickle nature of the common people.

  a Before Antony ascends to the Public Chair to make his oration, which remark typifies the commoners' dull-wittedness?

  b Whereas Brutus's speech appealed to the intellect, Antony's is emotional. He ends his opening remarks by choking back tears. How do the people react?

  c Marullus says of the commoners, "You blocks, you stones, you worse than senseless things" (*Act I Scene 1, line 36*). Antony says, "You are not wood, you are not stones, but men" (*Act III Scene 2, line 140*). Explain why Antony's oratorical approach shows a greater understanding of crowd pyschology.

  d Why does Antony mention the will to the crowd, but decline at first to read it?

  e Why does he
    i courteously ask permission to descend from the chair
    ii ask the commoners to "stand far off"?

  f Why does Antony call himself " a plain blunt man " and say he is "no orator, as Brutus is" (*lines 214–15*)?

  g The commoners forget the will till Antony reminds them of it (*line 236*). What does this tell us of their powers of concentration?

  h Why do the common people find the contents of the will so pleasing?

5 The commoners are shown at their most mindless and violent in *Act III Scene 3*:

  a At first they bully. How does this manifest itself?

  b Secondly they threaten physical violence. What is menacing about the reason given for this?

    c Lastly, they develop a macabre sense of humor. Which commoner is most responsible for this fatal twist?

6 The ordinary citizens of Rome can be referred to as "the people," "the commoners," "the crowd" or "the mob." Examine the scenes in which they either appear or are referred to, and decide which epithet is most appropriate in each case.

7 In what way is there a connection between the last lines of *Act III Scene 3* and the first lines of *Act IV Scene 1*?

# Close reading

Read the original Shakespeare and (if necessary) the modern transcription to gain an understanding of the speeches and extracts below. Then concentrate entirely on the original in answering the questions.

1 *Wherefore rejoice? What conquests brings he home?* (*Act I Scene 1, line 33*)

   a The speech contains a number of rhetorical questions – Marullus does not expect, or pause for, a spoken reply. Consider each question, and decide what mental response each member of the crowd would make.

   b Which of Marullus's lines indicates that he is a man of authority?

   c What is the force of his repeated use of "and"?

2 *I know that virtue to be in you, Brutus* (*Act I Scene 2, line 89*)

   a Cassius says "honour is the subject of my story." Is it?

   b Cassius opens by balancing Caesar's qualities against those of himself and Brutus. How does the blank verse reinforce this?

   c Caesar is quoted in Direct Speech three times. Do you think Cassius would change his voice when speaking these words? If so, how?

   d Cassius refers to an episode in Roman history to illustrate how he saved Caesar from drowning. Why is this unflattering to Caesar?

   e Which words of Cassius convey (i) his personal bitterness (ii) contempt (iii) incredulity (iv) frustration?

3 *Why, man, he doth bestride the narrow world | Like a Colossus* (*Act I Scene 2, lines 133–4*)

   a The Colossus of Rhodes (one of the seven wonders of the ancient world) was said to be 33–36 meters high. It was a statue in bronze of the sun-god Apollo, and ships entering the harbor passed between its legs. In Cassius's opening simile, which adjectives establish the scale of the image he is presenting?

240

b Which verbs also help the listener to imagine extremes of size?

c One adjective and one verb are linked together by alliteration – they have the same initial letter. Why is this so effective?

d Cassius continues by saying "Men at some time are masters of their fates," and refers to "stars" and "underlings." How does this link with his first sentence and continue to stretch the imagination of the listener?

e "Brutus and Caesar": this precedes a series of comparisons, which ends with "Brutus" at the beginning of a line and "Caesar" at the end of it. Can you detect other balances, in this section of the speech, and say how they are achieved?

f Rhetorical questions are used frequently here. Comment on (i) their effectiveness and (ii) their relationship to the exclamatory sentences (technically called "apostrophe").

g Read carefully the line "That her wide walks encompassed but one man." This is how it is printed in the 1623 Folio Edition. Since the "walks" of Rome might well have been wide, this edition of the original Shakespeare follows the Folio. Many editors, however, think "walks" is a misprint for "walls," because these "encompass" (i.e. encircle) a fortified city. This is reflected in the modern version. Which do you think Shakespeare originally intended?

h In Shakespeare's day, "Rome" was pronounced "Room"; "Roman" therefore sounded like "Roomman." Explain Cassius's pun.

4 *You are dull, Casca, and those sparks of life . . . (Act I Scene 3, line 57)*

a In the first line, what contrast is established in two particular words?

b What is the effect of the repeated used of the word "Why"? Is one used differently from the others?

    c "A man" is also repeated. Explain the effectiveness of this in terms of Cassius's argument.

    d Read the following speeches of Cassius. Repetition is a major feature. Identify where this occurs, and say whether it furthers the persuasiveness of Cassius in his appeal to Casca.

5 *It must be by his death* (*Act II Scene 1, line 10*)

    a Which words and phrases convey the impression that Brutus is thinking aloud?

    b There are two metaphors: one of the adder, one of the ladder.

      i Which is the principal one, and how do they inter-relate?

      ii Explain how each helps Brutus to come to a decision.

    c What is notable about the way Brutus expresses the outcome of his musings?

6 *Our course will seem too bloody, Caius Cassius* (*Act II Scene 1, line 162*)

    a Brutus says, "Let's be sacrificers, but not butchers, Caius." Collect together the expressions used by Brutus which are appropriate to butchery.

    b Brutus says that ideally they should be killing Caesar's spirit, not his body. Look up the words of Caesar's ghost in *Act IV Scene 3, lines 281, 282, 284*, and comment on the irony.

    c Brutus turns harsh words and phrases into softer ones, to make a savage act seem like a civilized one. How does he choose his words to achieve this?

    d How is Brutus's dismissal of Antony consistent in expression with his earlier imagery?

7 *O, pardon me, thou bleeding piece of earth* (*Act III Scene 1, line 254*)

    a Why is the corpse of Caesar called "a bleeding piece of earth"? Can you detect a biblical reference?

    b Caesar's wounds move Antony to develop an extended simile. Explain the effectiveness of "mouth," "lips" and "voice," sound and color.

    c How do blood, butchery, death and destruction become the recurrent themes of this speech?

**8** *Romans, countrymen and lovers (Act III Scene 2, line 13)*

    a This is a speech based on reason (unlike Antony's later, which is based on passion). Why does Brutus say the crowd should believe him?

    b How many words can you find that are antithetical (that is, in strong contrast), such as "less" / "more," "living"/ "dead"? What is the cumulative effect?

    c Many words and phrases are balanced: for example, "As Caesar loved me, I weep for him; as he was fortunate, I rejoice at it; as he was valiant, I honor him." Find more, and say why they are calculated to win over the crowd.

    d Two of the phrases so balanced stand out from the others and further the argument. Which are they?

    e There are three rhetorical questions leading up to "None, Brutus, none." Look at them carefully: what is significant about them all in terms of possible answers?

    f Which of Brutus's concluding sentences before Antony's appearance show that reason and balance are indeed his main platform and defense?

**9** *Friends, Romans, Countrymen, lend me your ears (Act III Scene 2, line 71)*

    a Antony uses the word " honourable" to describe Brutus and Cassius eight times. Each time the way in which it is spoken is different, and with a different purpose. Carefully trace the transition from the first "For Brutus was an honourable man" to "They that have done this deed are honourable," explaining how Antony's oratory has led the crowd from one point of view to another.

b In his second sentence, Antony says he is content to let Caesar's good points be buried with his bones. How many good points does he in fact make before this 35-line speech is ended?

c How does Antony deploy the words "ambition" and "ambitious" to win over the commoners to his point of view?

10 *But yesterday, the word of Caesar* . . . (*Act III Scene 2, line 116*)

a In Antony's first sentence, what word is designed to establish a personal relationship between Caesar and the common man?

b Why does Antony refer to the crowd as "masters"?

c How does he plant the idea of riot in the minds of the people in an indirect way?

d Why does he repeatedly use the word "wrong"?

e Having produced the will, one line of Antony's speech shows his subtlety in manipulating the crowd. Which is it?

11 *If you have tears, prepare to shed them now* (*Act III Scene 2, line 167*)

a Why does Antony begin by referring at some length to the first time Caesar wore his mantle?

b Why does he take each tear separately?

c Explain how Antony establishes that one particular stab-wound "was the most unkindest cut of all"?

d Antony's powers of oratory make the crowd weep. Why does he choose this point to let the sight of Caesar speak for itself?

12 *Good friends, sweet friends, let me not stir you up* (*Act III Scene 2, line 206*)

a This speech divides into two parts: at which point does Antony switch from one to another?

b How does he make insinuations against the conspirators without actually accusing them of anything?

c Why is he so self-deprecating about his skill as a speaker?

d Which adjectives are chosen by Antony to "speak" for him emotionally?

# Setting

1. In Shakespeare's day, plays were staged very simply. Apart from a few props and some simple costumes, the company had none of the resources which a professional company today would use to create an authentic atmosphere. In order to transport his audience from Elizabethan England to Ancient Rome, Shakespeare makes frequent reference to classical history, beliefs, politics and the geography of the period he is dramatizing. Here are some of the main ones, with one act and scene reference for each:

**Aeneas** Roman emperors were said to be descended from him. He rescued his father Anchises from the flames of Troy. (*Act I Scene 2*)

**Ate** The Roman goddess of revenge and strife. (*Act III Scene 1*)

**Augurers** Men who foretold the future by means of animals and birds, sometimes by examining their entrails. (*Act II Scene 4*)

**Capitol** The temple dedicated to Jupiter where Consuls took their vows of office, and to which generals were carried in triumph after military victories. (*Act II Scene 4*)

**Cato** Marcus Cato Uticensis, father of Portia. He committed suicide rather than surrender to Caesar. (*Act II Scene 1*) (His son, Young Cato, appears in Act IV Scenes 4 and 5 and dies fighting against Octavius Caesar.)

**Colossus** A huge statue, the legs of which bestrode the harbor entrance at Rhodes. (*Act I Scene 2*)

**Drachma** A small Greek coin, worth about 10 cents.

**Epicurus**  A Greek philosopher, born 341 B.C.; died 270 B.C. He taught that repose of the mind was the greatest good. Followers were accused of self-indulgence. (Stoics, on the other hand, believed that happiness lay in freedom from the bondage of human passions: they were therefore indifferent to hardship, pain and suffering.) (*Act V Scene 3*)

**Erebus**  The son of Chaos; the gloomy area through which all spirits had to pass on the way to Hades. (*Act II Scene 1*)

**Hybla**  A district in Sicily famous for beekeeping and honey. (*Act V Scene 3*)

**Ides of March**  March 15, according to the ancient Roman calendar. (*Act I Scene 2*)

**Lupercalia**  Games held annually on February 15, in honor of Pan, shepherd god of fertility. (*Act II Scene 3*)

**Nervii**  A tribe of the Belgae, which almost defeated the Roman army. (*Act III Scene 3*)

**Olympus**  The mountain in Greece where the Gods lived. (*Act III Scene 1*)

**Parthia**  A district in northeast Iran. (*Act V Scene 3*)

**Philippi**  A district in Macedonia. (*Act IV Scene 3*)

**Plutus**  God of wealth. (*Act IV Scene 3*)

**Pompey**  Gnaeus Pompeius (106–48 B.C.). At first an ally of Julius Caesar, but later a rival. Defeated by Caesar in 48 B.C. He sailed for Egypt, but was assassinated on his arrival there. He built a theater in Rome which held several thousand spectators. Its porch had one hundred marble columns. (*Act I Scene 1*)

**Praetors**  Roman judges in civil law. (*Act I Scene 3*)

**Sardis** A district in Asia Minor. (*Act IV Scene 3*)

**Senate** The legislative council of Ancient Rome. (*Act I Scene 3*)

**Tarquins** Two kings of Rome in the sixth century B.C. The second, Tarquinius Superbus, was hated for his tyrannical and arrogant rule; he was expelled by Lucius Junius Brutus in 509 B.C. (*Act II Scene 1*)

**Tiber** The river of Rome. (*Act I Scene 2*)

**Triumvirs** An association of three men, ruling Rome as an equal partnership. (*Act IV Scene 1*)

**Tribunes** Representatives of the common people, elected to protect their interests. (*Act I Scene 1*)
  a Trace each to its context.
  b Explain their dramatic significance in terms of
    i plot and/or
    ii setting/atmosphere.

2 Because strict accuracy of detail was not of major importance to an Elizabethan audience, Shakespeare's Roman plays often contain anachronisms – for example, a clock strikes twice in the play, and clocks were not invented until the fourteenth century.
  a Find three references to clocks in the play. (*Act II Scene 1, Act II Scene 4, Act V Scene 3*) Explain why time is relevant to the dramatic development of the play at each of these points.
  b How can you tell from references to dress in the following scenes that the Elizabethan actors were not dressed as Romans?
    i *Act I Scene 2*
    ii *Act II Scene 1*
  c In *Act I Scene 3* there is a reference to Elizabethan theatergoing practice, which would not have applied in Roman times. Can you find it?

# Examination questions

1. How does Shakespeare handle the themes of honor, loyalty and enmity in *Julius Caesar*?

2. "Caesar's murder was unjustified: it was the most appalling of Brutus's many blunders." Consider and discuss the implications of this statement.

3. "In *Julius Caesar*, the tension is created by placing Duty in conflict with Friendship." Is this an adequate explanation for the dramatic appeal of the play?

4. Portia says she possesses "a man's mind but a woman's might." What, therefore, are her problems, and how well does she cope with them?

5. By what means does Cassius persuade Brutus and Casca to join the conspiracy? What is thereby shown of his character and motives?

6. "Brutus destroys himself by trying to impose an ideal on the actual." Discuss.

7. Show how superstition and the supernatural play an important part in the dramatic development of *Julius Caesar*.

8. How does Shakespeare distinguish between the two wives who play a part in *Julius Caesar*? Which has the closer relationship with her husband?

9. It has been said that "Shakespeare despised a mob." Do you think that this is reflected in his handling of historic fact in *Julius Caesar*?

10. "The dominant character in the play is Caesar, notwithstanding the fact that he dies in Act Three." Discuss.

11 With reference to his dealings with Brutus and Caesar, identify the main features of Antony's character.

12 In what ways does the character of Cassius change after the murder of Caesar?

13 Is there a case for saying that *The Tragedy of Julius Caesar* should be retitled *The Tragedy of Marcus Brutus*?

14 Trace carefully the steps by which Antony sways the mob in the funeral scene, Act III Scene 2.

15 "Pompous and contemptible at times, perhaps; but though his greatness dims, it is never entirely extinguished." Do you agree with this assessment of Caesar?

16 "It is the personality of Brutus that attracts our chief sympathy and concern." Is Brutus worthy of this critical approach?

17 "His demeanour is intolerable." Is this a fair comment on Brutus's behavior in the quarrel scene with Cassius?

18 What do we learn of Antony's character from (a) his encounter with the conspirators immediately after the assassination, (b) when he is alone with Caesar's body and (c) when he is in conference with Octavius and Lepidus?

19 "The first four acts of *Julius Caesar* are based on talk; the fifth on action." How does Shakespeare show his skill in both aspects of his dramatic art?

20 The entry of Antony's servant in *Act III Scene 1* has been identified by several critics as the turning point in the play. Why should this be so?

21 Explain why Brutus exclaims, "O, Julius Caesar, thou art mighty yet" when in fact he has been defeated in battle by Antony and Octavius.

22 Give an account of the meeting of the Triumvirate in *Act IV Scene 1*, pointing out what new aspects of Antony's character emerge from it, and making any cross-references to his funeral speeches which seem apt and illuminating.

23  In what ways do the characters of Brutus and Cassius differ? Show how these differences reveal themselves in any scene or part of a scene in which they appear together.

24  "*Julius Caesar* is a play of Conflict and of Tension." Show how these two qualities are best illustrated by reference to scenes in which they are of major dramatic significance.

25  "Shakespeare's Caesar is loved and honored by both Brutus and Cassius. As portrayed in the play, he is unworthy of it." Discuss, with particular reference to his speeches and actions (a) at the feast of Lupercal and (b) on the morning of his assassination.

26  Outline the progress of the battles fought at Philippi, and explain how Shakespeare overcomes the problem of staging them.

27  "It must not be supposed that in creating the major characters of *Julius Caesar*, Shakespeare neglected the minor ones." Which three minor characters best illustrate this critical opinion?

28  Compare Brutus and Antony as mob orators.

29  *Julius Caesar* has been called "a political thriller." In what ways is such a description justified?

30  By what means does Shakespeare transport his Elizabethan audience to the streets and homes of Ancient Rome?

# One-word-answer quiz

1 Who stabbed Caesar first?

2 At the base of whose statue did Caesar fall?

3 Where did Antony find Caesar's will?

4 What was Lucius looking for when he found a "sealed up" paper?

5 Who was "meet to be sent on errands"?

6 With which star did Caesar compare himself?

7 What couldn't the augurers find, when they examined their sacrifice?

8 What was the name of Antony's sister's son?

9 Where did Portia wound herself to prove her constancy?

10 In which river did Cassius swim with Caesar?

11 Who would "never follow anything that other men begin"?

12 Who drew Antony to one side before the assassination?

13 Who swallowed fire, and died?

14 Who did Cassius recognize by his gait?

15 Who stood "quite confounded" after Caesar's death?

16 Who was the last conspirator to shake hands with Antony?

17 How many times was Caesar stabbed?

18 How many senators did Brutus think had been put to death?

19 How many "ghastly women" did Casca see near the Capitol?

20 How many drachmas did Caesar leave each Roman citizen?

21 How many spouts did the bleeding fountain have?

22 Which side of the battlefield did Octavius fight on?

23 Which town was famous for its bees?

24 What was the trade of the "mender of bad soles"?

25 What is "young ambition's ladder," according to Brutus?

26 Was Cinna the Poet a married man?

27 Who took bribes from the Sardians?

28 In which ear was Caesar deaf?

29 On whose birthday was the battle of Philippi fought?

30 How many leagues from Rome was Octavius on the day of Caesar's murder?

31 At what hour did the clock strike during Brutus's meeting with the conspirators?

32 At what time did the conspirators meet Caesar on the ides of March?

33 At what time did Portia speak to the soothsayer?

34 At what time did Brutus decide to attempt a second battle?

35 Who spoke well of Pompey, to Caesar's annoyance?

36 Which former king of Rome was expelled from the city?

37 How many times did Calpurnia cry out "Help, ho! they murder Caesar"?

38 Who held the sword while Brutus ran upon it?

39 Where was Caesar when he suffered from a fever?

40 Whose eyes were ferret-like and fiery?

41 Who was "quick mettle" when he was at school?

42 What was the name of Portia's father?

43 Who wished that Cassius's enterprise might thrive?

44 Where was the dead body of Cassius sent for burial?

45 Who die many times before their deaths, according to Caesar?

46 On which feast day was it the custom for runners to touch barren women?

47 How many times was Caesar offered the crown?

48 Who was described as "but a limb of Caesar"?

49 Whose sight "was ever thick"?

50 What was Caius Ligarius wearing to signify his illness?

# What's missing?

Complete the following quotations:

1   The fault, dear Brutus, is . . .
2   You blocks, you stones . . .
3   Caesar should be a beast without a heart / If . . .
4   What touches us ourself shall . . .
5   I had rather be a dog . . .
6   All the conspirators save only he . . .
7   What need we any spur but our own cause . . .?
8   You are my true and honourable wife, / As dear to me as . . .
9   I rather choose to wrong the dead, to wrong myself and you, than . . .
10  A peevish schoolboy, worthless of such honour, . . .
11  Such men as he be never at heart's ease . . .
12  The cause is in my will, . . .
13  The evil that men do lives after them; . . .
14  Will you be pricked in number of our friends, / Or . . .
15  When Caesar says ' . . .' it is performed.
16  If we do meet again, why . . .; / If not . . .
17  Since Cassius first did whet me against Caesar . . .
18  I had as lief not be, as live to be . . .
19  That you do love me, I am nothing jealous . . .
20  Thrice hath Calpurnia in her sleep cried out ' . . .'
21  Three parts of him / Is ours already . . .
22  These growing feathers, . . ., will make him fly an ordinary pitch.
23  I have a man's mind . . .

24 Brutus had rather be a villager / Than . . .

25 Cowards die . . .

26 But when I tell him he hates flatterers . . .

27 Hence, home, you idle creatures . . .

28 Caesar shall forth . . .

29 I am not gamesome; I do lack . . . that is in Antony

30 There is but one mind in all these men, and . . .

31 Well, Brutus, thou art noble; yet I see . . .

32 If you have tears . . .

33 This is a slight, unmeritable man . . .

34 But 'tis a common proof that lowliness . . .

35 Oh, pardon me, thou bleeding piece of earth . . .

36 I, that denied thee gold, will . . .

37 Friends, I owe more tears to . . .

38 There is tears for his love; joy for his fortune; . . .

39 It is the bright day that brings forth the adder . . .

40 There is a tide in the affairs of men . . .

41 Let's be sacrificers, but not . . ., Caius.

42 In such a time as this, it is not meet . . .

43 My heart doth joy that yet in all my life . . .

44 Look, with a spot . . .

45 Why, man, he doth bestride the narrow world like . . .

46 Stoop, Romans, stoop, And let us . . .

47 Three or four wenches, where I stood, cried . . .

48 You are dull, Casca, and . . .

49 I am as constant as . . .

50 Let me have men about me that . . .